P9-BYC-331

*To
the flesh
of
my flesh*

TABLE of CONTENTS

Foreword vii

Author's Note ix

Acknowledgments xi

1. A Firm Foundation.................................. 1

2. Where It All Began 10

3. The Character of Man before Sin..................... 19

4. The Character of Man in Sin 27

5. The Character of Man Redeemed by Christ 37

6. The Non-Christian Point of View 44

7. The Christian Point of View 51

8. Attitudes and Actions 62

9. Popular Tactics 72

10. Structure of a Biblical Defense 81

11. Defending the Faith (1)............................. 99

12. Defending the Faith (2)............................. 111

13. Defending the Faith (3)............................. 123

14. An Apologetic Parable 133

FOREWORD

John M. Frame
Associate Professor of Apologetics and Systematic Theology
Westminster Theological Seminary

Richard Pratt has accomplished a great deal for one so young. Though not yet a seminary graduate, he has been a pastor for several years. He is working in the Honors Program (reserved for our brightest students) at Westminster Seminary. Now he has written a book aimed at training young people to be apologists— a book tested out among the young people of the church which he pastored. The book is excellent in many ways, and it gives us grounds for expecting more fine work from its author in the future.

The volume is particularly welcome for three reasons. First, it presents Reformed (or "Van Tillian") apologetics in genuinely popular language. That task has been tried before, but most of the earlier "popularizations" have lapsed at crucial points into philosophical language, and annoyingly unclear philosophical language at that. Part of the problem has been the myth that one cannot accurately expound Van Til without using Van Til's own terminology—a myth that has greatly inhibited the dissemination, acceptance and use of Van Til's insights. In this respect, Mr. Pratt's book is something of a breakthrough. I would expect and hope that this accomplishment will give the book a wide hearing.

Second, the book is not an exposition of Van Til's thought (of which there are plenty), but a *training manual.* Reformed people have been generally weak in *training* one another to *do* apologetics. Generally we have set forth the theory and have hoped that the practice would take care of itself. But this attitude has often kept Reformed apologetics in the status of a scholars' game. That ought not to be. Van Til's insights are life-transforming and world-transforming. It is time that gifted apologists be mobilized to press the claims of Scripture upon their friends and neighbors and upon the whole opinion-making process of our culture.

Finally, the book is directed to *high school students!* I found it hard to believe that anyone would try to teach Reformed apologetics at that level, but Mr. Pratt actually brings it off. His gift of communication to young people is quite extraordinary. He has proved that it can be done. And certainly if it *can* be done, it *ought* to be done. The high school years are the ideal time to become clear on what one believes and why he believes it. These are the years when the great questions emerge in forms suited to intelligent discussion. High schoolers are often highly interested in nailing down the "whys" of the Christian faith, and they can evangelize their friends with enormous enthusiasm and effectiveness. Many of us can testify that the Bible really came alive to us for the first time during this period, that we then really came to see that Christianity is *true* and we first became deeply concerned about friends who did not know Christ as Lord and Savior. Apologetic discussions take on a unique kind of excitement at that age. The church loses much if it fails to harness that enthusiasm and the great abilities of its young people.

Therefore, I am very pleased indeed to see the publication of *Every Thought Captive.* It could mark the transition of Reformed apologetics from the seminary classroom, not only to the high school, but to the world. May our sovereign God bring that to pass.

AUTHOR'S NOTE

In II Corinthians 10:5 the apostle Paul describes his task as an apostle saying,

> We are destroying speculations and every lofty thing raised up against the knowledge of God, and we are taking every thought captive to the obedience of Christ.

In these few words Paul sets forth two goals which I have adopted as the basis for this manual. As those who love God and His Word, believers in Christ are to be "destroying speculations and every lofty thing raised up against the knowledge of God." Unbelievers try with great persistence to replace the knowledge of God with some other notion. Yet, because Christians are aware of the importance of acknowledging God in all areas of life, they are committed to challenging and destroying those substitutes. Loving God compels us to destroy all idols produced by men. Moreover, believers aware of their task do not seek merely to discredit the corruption of disbelief. They also make it their practice to be "taking every thought captive to the obedience of Christ." Non-Christians are in need of salvation from the presence and consequences of sin and rebellion against God. This salvation comes only through whole-hearted belief in and commitment to Christ. When such commitment is made, the thinking of the one who was once an enemy of God becomes submitted to the "obedience of Christ." In the pages which follow I have sought to direct the believer in this twofold task. Believers are engaged in a warfare in which all is at stake. We must, therefore, destroy speculations exposing their emptiness and futility and we must complete our task by taking *Every Thought Captive.*

With the numerous works on the subject of Christian apologetics already in publication, it seems that some justification should be given for the addition of still another. This manual is certainly not accounted for because of its originality. It has not been my intention to devise a new or unique approach to the defense of Christianity. It is apparent with only a cursory reading that I am indebted to the work of Dr. Cornelius Van Til. My dependence on his many volumes is so great that noting particular cases would be superfluous. As a footnote to this entire effort I acknowledge Dr. Van Til, undoubtedly the greatest defender of the Christian faith in our century.

If this manual earns its standing on the bookshelf, it does so because it is intended to be thoroughly biblical in its approach and popular in its presentation. I have always been concerned with the fact that the most worthwhile writings on the subject at hand have been beyond the grasp of the average layperson. Aiming at this level, I hope to have simplified and clarified the basic elements of a biblical defense of Christianity for the large majority of my fellow believers.

The manual is divided into thirteen lessons of instruction and a fourteenth lesson of practical illustration. This arrangement was made so that the lessons could be used in a Sunday school or Bible study program. Each lesson builds upon the preceding lessons and should be studied in sequence. Review questions are included at the end of each lesson for reflection and discussion.

My hopes for these lessons are many. I pray that they may be used to bring the gospel of Christ to unbelievers in an effective and convincing manner. Moreover, I desire to see them used to strengthen and encourage believers to confidence and boldness in the proclamation of salvation in Christ. Finally, because the presentation is suited for the uninitiated, I hope that one far more capable than I will be introduced to the defense of Christianity by these lessons and will then go further in the years to come and teach us all how we might better take *Every Thought Captive.*

R.L.P.

ACKNOWLEDGMENTS

There are many who have contributed to the composition of this manual. I especially thank Dr. Cornelius Van Til whose work has become a milestone in the history of the church. I also acknowledge Mr. John Frame whose interpretation of Van Til is incisive, creative, and greatly needed. Moreover, I give appreciation to Dr. Jack L. Arnold, whose pastoral gifts have meant so much to me through my years of study as a Christian. Finally, I thank Mr. Bobby Dobyns for his work on the cover and illustrations, and the numerous proofreaders and typists who have given freely of their time and effort.

Lesson 1. A Firm Foundation

> Sanctify Christ as Lord in your hearts, always being ready to make a defense to everyone who asks you to give an account for the hope that is in you (I Pet. 3:15).

A life of obedience to the Bible is like a house built on a firm foundation. At the close of His Sermon on the Mount, Jesus said:

> Therefore every one who hears these words of Mine, and acts upon them, may be compared to a wise man, who built his house upon the rock; And the rain descended, and the floods came, and the winds blew, and burst against that house; and yet it did not fall; for it had been founded upon the rock. And every one who hears these words of Mine, and does not act upon them, will be like a foolish man, who built his house upon the sand. And the rain descended, and the floods came, and the winds blew, and burst against that house; and it fell, and great was its fall (Matt. 7:24–27).

Jesus pointed to the obvious fact that the strength of a foundation determines the ability of a house to withstand heavy rains and strong winds. If a man builds his house on sand, it will fall; but if he builds his dwelling on solid rock, it will stand secure even in a fierce storm. In these lessons, we will seek to build a house. And, as the rains and winds of unbelief assault our house, we will rest assured knowing that our groundwork is the solid rock of the Word of Christ.

Yet, even before we can lay a foundation, it is best to know what sort of "house" we are going to build. Let us, then, begin with this basic consideration.

A. The "House of Apologetics"

The term "apologetics" is often misunderstood. Usually it brings to mind the times when we wronged a friend or loved one and found it necessary to return to him saying "I'm sorry." Though this is the way "apology"is used in ordinary conversation, it will be used in a more restricted, technical sense in these lessons. The word "apologetics" is within a family of related words (apology, apologize, etc.) derived from the Greek APOLOGIA, a word which is used quite often in pagan and Christian literature and in the New Testament itself. The *Apology of Socrates* is an account of the *defense* which he offered before the court of Athens. Justin Martyr, in his *Apology*, sought to *defend* his fellow Christians against the false accusations which were hurled at them by the unbelieving world. When Paul stood before the mob in Jerusalem, he said, "hear my *defense* (APOLOGIA) which I now offer to you" (Acts 22:1). To "apologize," in this sense means to offer a defense; an "apology" is a defense offered; and "apologetics" is the study which pertains directly to the development and use of a defense.

In one way or another, apologetics is an area of concern for many religions and philosophies in the world. Yet, in these lessons attention will be given only to the defense of Christian truth as it has been revealed to man in the Scriptures of the Old and New Testaments. This sort of apologetics is called "Christian apologetics" for it is "the vindication of the Christian philosophy of life against the various forms of non-Christian philosophy of life."[1] We are not concerned with apologetics in general but with apologetics of a particular sort. To put it in terms of the analogy used previously, the house which we are seeking to build in these lessons is the house of Christian apologetics.

B. The Meaning of "Biblical Apologetics"

When Jesus spoke of the sure foundation which should lie beneath every area of our lives, He had something particular in mind. He said that the only foundation which can give us the strength needed to withstand the raging storms of sin and

[1]Cornelius Van Til, *Apologetics* (Class syllabus), p. 1.

Figure 1

destruction is His Word. The Scripture of the Old and New Testaments is the very Word of God. It is the common confession of all Christians that:

> All Scripture is inspired by God and profitable for teaching, for reproof, for correction, for training in righteousness; that the man of God may be adequate, equipped for every good work (II Tim. 3:16, 17).

The Bible is the absolutely authoritative guide for all believers; without it we are left merely guessing at God's mind, but with it God's directives for all areas of our lives are made certain and clear. So with the Psalmist we may say:

> Thy word is a lamp to my feet, and a light to my path (Ps. 119:105).

It was in this way that Jesus referred to His spoken word which confirmed the written Word at every point as the very foundation upon which we must build. The Bible is the foundation without which all our endeavors will crumble into ruin (see Fig. 1).

It is not a complete picture to say that the Bible acts merely as a foundation for apologetics, for even the inexperienced believer can see that its authority is one of the most important of his beliefs in need of defense. A great many attacks on the Christian faith are aimed at the Bible. The Bible is often accused of containing errors and having little or no more authority than any other writing. Because it is often necessary to defend belief in the Scriptures, the relation of apologetics to the Bible is sometimes

Figure 2

misunderstood. The Bible is both the foundation upon which our defense must be built and one of our beliefs which must be defended. All too often, this twofold role which the Bible must play is forgotten. Well-meaning Christians lose sight of the foundational character of the Bible and tend to build their defense on mere human wisdom and reasoning. The Word is placed, as it were, on the roof of their structure and is supported by apologetics. Yet, the difficulty of supporting the Scriptures with a structure resting on human wisdom as its ultimate authority often becomes too great. The builders of such a house may close their eyes and claim otherwise, but destruction is as inevitable for that house as for a house built on sand (see Fig. 2).

As followers of Christ, we must remember always to build our defense of the Christian faith on the sure foundation of the Bible. If we do so, there will be no weight too great to be supported; no wind too strong to be resisted.

Biblical apologetics can be compared, therefore, to the relation of a king and his generals. It is clearly the generals' responsibility to defend their king, even as apologetics defends the Bible. Yet, it is equally true that honorable generals defend their king according to the commands and directives of the king himself. Even so, apologetics must defend the Bible while submitting entirely to the defensive principles and directives revealed there.

This guiding role of the Bible for apologetics can be seen clearly in I Peter 3:15. "But sanctify Christ as Lord in your hearts, always being ready to make a defense to every one who asks you to give an account for the hope that is in you, yet with gentleness and reverence." In the preceding context, Peter writes about the sufferings through which every Christian must go. He knows that times of suffering the attacks of the sinful world are often occasions for forgetting that we serve Christ and that He must be obeyed and trusted throughout every trial. Since Peter hopes his readers will give a proper response to the questions their oppressors may ask, he instructs them to prepare for their suffering by acquiring a proper attitude toward Christ. Care must be taken to see the order in which the portions of this verse were written. First, Peter says, "Sanctify Christ as Lord in your hearts," and then he adds, "always being ready to make a defense. . . ." Before a defense should be made, Christ must be set apart as the Lord, the one who governs and rules our lives in every area. Notice that we are to set Christ apart as Lord in our *hearts*. This does not mean, as we may be tempted to think by our modern conceptions, that merely our emotional stability should rest in Christ while our reason is free to do as it pleases in apologetics. Nor does it mean that Christ's Lordship should remain only deep inside us, never affecting our answers to the world's questions. The Scriptures teach that the heart is the center of the personality out of which "flow the springs of life" (Prov. 4:23). What we do in our hearts governs not only our emotions, but our reason and every other aspect of our lives as well. Moreover, to sanctify Christ as Lord in the heart means that His Lordship will also be effective in all our outward functions, including the defending of our faith. So, according to Peter, submission to the authority of Christ is necessary for a proper defense. As our Lord, Christ leads us as we defend the faith. This guidance comes through His Word, and without such guidance, all is vain.

In the lessons which follow, we will be concerned with establishing an apology for the Christian faith securely based on the solid rock of the Bible. There are scores of books, some better than others, which offer different approaches to defending Christian truth. This great variety often leaves the Christian confused. Yet, in all this confusion, one thing remains clear. Rather than adopting an approach to apologetics because famous men use it, because of its apparent numerical success, or the strength it may have given our personal faith, we must cleave to the approach which is according to the principles of the Bible. If we desire a defense which will stand and never fall, we must build it on the Word of God.

C. The Importance of Apologetics

The study of apologetics and the development of the ability to rightly defend Christian truth is the responsibility of every believer. From the oldest to the youngest, richest to poorest, from the genius to the simple-minded, everyone who has trusted in Christ for salvation is under obligation to study apologetics. Yet, well-meaning Christians often fail to take this responsibility seriously.

One popular reason for neglecting apologetics rests on a misunderstanding of one of the sayings of Jesus found in Matthew 10:19.

> But when they deliver you up, do not become anxious about how or what you will speak; for it shall be given you in that hour what you are to speak. For it is not you who speak, but it is the Spirit of your Father who speaks in you.

Serious misunderstandings have risen from this passage, especially from the King James translation *"give no thought* how or what ye shall speak." It is often said that this passage teaches that full reliance on the Holy Spirit for guidance when defending the faith rules out all need for preparatory study. In fact, it is believed that the study of apologetics shows a lack of faith and true submission to God. Yet, such an interpretation of this passage does not do justice either to a careful examination of the passage itself or to the rest of Scripture.

To begin with, Jesus is not saying "do not think about what you will say," as the King James translation indicates to our modern ears. Instead, as the more recent translations show, Jesus is warning against anxiety and worry. In the verses which precede Matthew 10:19, Jesus says that His apostles will be taken before governors and kings. Coming before such great men could be a frightening experience, but Jesus encourages the disciples beforehand against worry and fear. All fear should be gone from those who defend the faith because they will never stand alone. Jesus says that the Holy Spirit of God will give them strength and wisdom in their times of need. As Paul said, "at my first defense no one supported me . . . but the Lord stood with me, and strengthened me . . . " (II Tim. 4:16, 17). It is important, however, to know that this strengthening work of the Spirit is not a substitute for faithful study and preparation. Though we are warned not to worry about food and clothing (cf. Matt. 6:25ff.), we are nevertheless commanded to work and to earn these things. In the same way, we must also fulfill our responsibility of preparation. Peter wrote that we should "always be ready (prepared) to make a defense" (I Pet. 3:15). So, he who is lax in these matters fails to submit to the Lordship of Christ and to depend on the Holy Spirit, for true submission and reliance will result in the careful study of apologetics.

Another reason often given for neglecting the study of apologetics is that defending the faith is the job of the so-called professionals, not the average Christian layman. Teachers and ministers are expected to have a carefully devised defense but apologetics is thought to be too philosophical, abstract, and impractical for the layman. Even many who recognize the responsibility of the layman in evangelism think that they should only share the gospel and then refer anyone who has a question about the credibility of the Christian faith to their pastor, the "expert." While it is true that ministers and teachers have a heavier responsibility in apologetics than most believers, every believer has the duty of defending the faith. I Peter 3:15, a passage we have already seen, makes no exceptions. Everyone is to suffer for Christ and everyone is to be ready to defend his hope in Christ.

Moreover, Paul makes it clear that every believer should be defending the faith. As an apostle, Paul was especially "appointed for the defense of the gospel" (Phil. 1:16). Yet, Paul knew that the job of apologetics was not his responsibility alone. So, he said to the Philippians:

> . . . I have you in my heart, since both in my imprisonment and in the defense and confirmation of the gospel you are all partakers of grace with me (Phil. 1:7).

Paul had been imprisoned for his preaching of the gospel, but the Philippian Christians did not desert him. They had sent him gifts by representatives of their church. In fact, they had become so involved in Paul's ministry as an apostle that they, too, were "experiencing the same" (1:30) as he. One aspect of their sharing with Paul is described as "the defense and confirmation of the gospel" (1:7). The Philippians were commended because they took seriously the job of defending the Christian faith. So it is that everyone who shares in the defense of Christianity stands commended by the Word of God. Apologetics is not for just a few; it is for everyone.

The importance of apologetics can be seen in many other ways. An ability to defend our beliefs will make our evangelism more effective. We do not have to fear bringing up the subject of Christianity with our friends and neighbors if we are able to give answers to their questions. We need never fear the highly intelligent unbeliever if we are able to defend the faith. Evangelistic zeal is increased by the study of apologetics. Moreover, the one who hears the gospel can often have his doubts cleared up by hearing the correct answer to his questions. Beyond this, a biblical apologetic strengthens the believer's faith. Many Christians are plagued by recurring doubts. These doubts often cause the believer to fall short of his potential ability to serve Christ. Apologetics enables the believer to ward off many of the temptations toward infidelity he may experience. This ability will in turn make it possible for him to pay attention to other matters of learning and service. Even the Christian who never experiences problems with doubt can gain the added confidence and enthusiasm necessary to be a more obedient child of God by a thorough study of apologetics. Apologetics is a subject of great importance for all and should be of great interest to all.

In the lessons which follow, we will be building, brick by brick, this important house of apologetics, resting it firmly on the Word of God. As we do so, there is but one hope: that believers will be better equipped to serve their Lord and to build up His kingdom by obedience to Him and by the effective winning of the lost.

Review Questions

1. What is the meaning of "Christian Apologetics" as the term will be used in these lessons?
2. Describe the twofold relationship between the Bible and apologetics.

3. What are two objections often raised against the study of apologetics? How would you answer these objections?
4. What are some personal benefits you should derive from studying apologetics?
5. Point out several ways in which I Peter 3:15 relates directly to the study of apologetics.

Lesson 2. Where It All Began

> In the beginning God created the heavens and the earth (Gen. 1:1).

In the preceding lesson we saw how the Bible relates to our defense of the Christian faith. We must develop our defense only as we study the Bible and apply the principles found there to our procedure. If we are going to follow through with this perspective, there will be several matters which will need to be discussed, beginning with a look at the biblical concept of creation.

A. God and His Creation

It is certainly not insignificant that the Bible begins with an uncompromising declaration of God as the Creator of all. The Bible is a religious book designed to show the way of true religion and as such, makes clear in its opening statements the importance of recognizing God as the Creator of all things. It is not going too far to say that the whole Bible elaborates on this one theme of God as the Creator and Lord. Man could never have lived in the garden before sin, the fall of man into sin could have never occurred, and the salvation accomplished by the death and resurrection of Jesus would be senseless if there had been no creation by God. Eden was the harmonious relation between God and His creation. Sin is the rebellion of creatures against their Creator. Salvation is deliverance from sin and the right-standing of the creature before God. John speaks of this fundamental character of God's creative activity saying, "all things came into being through Him; and apart from Him nothing came into being that has come into being" (John 1:3).

When we think even for a moment about Genesis 1:1, we recognize that the act of creation forms a basic division. On the one hand there is the One who created, and on the other hand, there is that which He created. Consequently, a distinction is made between God the Creator and God's creation. We shall call this the "Creator-creature distinction" for it is a concept which must be explored further and to which reference will often be made. This distinction between the Creator and His creatures must never be forgotten nor set aside for even a moment for it is indispensable to the development of biblical apologetics.

1. *God, Independent of All*

Christians today seldom think of God as anything more than an old grandfather who sits in the clouds helplessly watching disappointing events occurring on earth below Him. God is thought to be practically useless and unimportant to the world except when men have whims and wishes they want fulfilled by Him. In the minds of many people, God is dispensable to the world process. "He is needed only in times of disaster and personal trauma," they say. Moreover, God Himself is often thought somehow to be dependent on His creation. He wishes things could be different than they are and is often taken by surprise by clever men. As much as this sort of thinking has grown in the church, it is nevertheless far from the biblical picture of God. God is not a dependent "sugar-daddy"; He is the all-powerful Creator and constant sustainer of all things. Romans 11:36 speaks to this effect:

> For from Him and through Him and to Him are all things.

A close look will reveal the great wealth of the knowledge of God packed into this passage. First, Paul says that the whole creation is "from Him." In other words, God created it out of nothing; the creation did not come into existence on its own. Lastly, he says that creation is "to Him," that is, for God's ultimate glory and pleasure, not for man's or any other creature's. Even so, the second description of creation given here is also instructive. Creation is "through Him." Here Paul does not speak of how God related to the creation at the beginning, nor what His position will be at the end. He speaks of God as the One who sustains and upholds His creation every moment. The creation continues its existence through God. The basic point is this: As God was the creating power in the beginning, He is the sustaining power now.

In the same way, as God was not created by the creation, He is not now in any way sustained by His creation. In Acts 17:25 we read:

> neither is He [God] served by human hands, as though He needed anything, since He Himself gives to all life and breath and all things.

Plainly enough, God does not need anything that must or can be filled by the creation, for in reality the very opposite is the case. All the needs of creation are filled by God. God is, in this sense, *independent.*

2. Creation, Dependent on God

While we may speak of God as independent of His creation, we must affirm as well the total dependence of creation on God. We know that children depend on their parents but as they grow older, they need their parents' care less and less. Even a newborn infant is able to survive for a short while without his parents. This is not, however, the sort of dependence creation has on God. Creation cannot, even for a moment in the slightest way, exist apart from God's sustaining power. The Scriptures speak to this effect on several occasions.

> . . . He Himself gives to *all* life and breath and *all things* (Acts 17:25).

> He is before *all things,* and in Him *all things* hold together (Col. 1:17).

God binds, provides, and sustains all things without exception. From the greatest to the smallest, every aspect of creation is entirely dependent on God for its continuing existence. We must agree with John Calvin that belief in God as the Creator must be coupled with belief in Him as the controlling Lord of history. The world cannot continue on its own power. All existence is from and through God. Indeed, we must think of creation as entirely *dependent* on God (see Fig. 3).

We will see in the lessons which follow that the recognition of this distinction between the independent God and dependent creation is one of the fundamental differences between Christians and non-Christians. Christians strive to see everything in light of creation's dependence on God while the non-Christian tries to

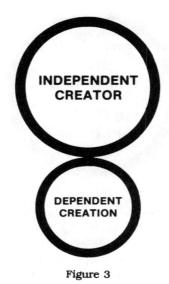

Figure 3

deny creation's dependence. As strongly as it may be denied by some non-Christians, in one way or another, every person who has not trusted in Christ for salvation fails to account for the Creator-creature distinction and somehow puts God and His creation in mutual dependence on each other and ascribes to creation a degree of independence. With all the diversity of opinion among non-Christians, this is one uniting factor: the Creator-creature distinction is denied (see Fig. 4).

3. God Revealed to Man

While we must insist as Christians on the maintenance of the distinction between God and the creation, we must never forget that God has revealed Himself and His will to man. Though God has adopted various ways of revealing Himself at different times, we will give attention to the two basic ways in which He has chosen to reveal Himself in all ages.

a. Every Aspect of Creation

God has so marvelously constructed the created universe that every portion of it reveals Him to man. Every element of the world without exception discloses God and His will to man.

Figure 4

The heavens are telling of the glory of God; and the firmament is declaring the work of His hands. Day to day pours forth speech, and night to night reveals knowledge (Ps. 19:1-2).

The creation, in all its splendor, makes known the glorious qualities of God and the righteous demands which He makes of man. As Paul has said:

> For since the creation of the world His invisible attributes, His eternal power and divine nature, have been clearly seen, being understood through what has been made, . . . they know the ordinance of God . . . (Rom. 1:20, 32).

Though fallen men deny it and Christians often have difficulty seeing it, the Bible teaches plainly that all men have God clearly revealed to them through every aspect of creation, even their own personal makeup. God's disclosure is unavoidable. We cannot know one aspect of creation without being turned toward its Creator. "The heavens declare His righteousness, and all the peoples have seen His glory" (Ps. 97:6).

Man can understand himself and the creation surrounding him only as he recognizes the Creator-creature distinction revealed there and sees the will of God more clearly through his observation of creation. For example, it is not enough to know that cows eat grass. True apprehension of cows and grass reveals the providential power and care of God and the task which was given to man to subdue every other creature to God's glory (cf. Gen. 1:28). The distance between the earth and her nearest star is truly understood only as its disclosure of God is recognized, for the multiple light years of distance is the mere work of God's fingers and displays to man his need for humility before God and thanksgiving for His grace (cf. Ps. 8:1–5). As creation cannot exist apart from God, it cannot be silent of God. The more fully one apprehends any fact of the universe, the more it will reveal God and His will to him.

b. Special Revelations of God

God has for various reasons always seen fit to accompany His revelation in all of creation with special revelations of Himself. In the garden of Eden, He spoke audibly to Adam about the tree of the knowledge of good and evil. To the patriarchs, God disclosed Himself in dreams, appearances, and visions. To Moses, God spoke in a burning bush and on tablets of stone. To the apostles, He spoke through the life and words of Jesus, His Son. For our time, God has spoken by the inspired Scriptures.

The use of particular aspects of creation for revelation has been intended to supplement in one way or another the revealing quality of the rest of creation. Before sin came into the world, man's obedience was tested by special revelation. After the fall, special disclosures had the twofold purpose of showing the way of salvation in Christ and helping man to understand better the revelation of God and His will in all other aspects of creation. Sin has placed man under judgment and blinded him to true awareness of God revealed in all creation. As a result, the Scriptures stand as a means by which we may understand ourselves, the world, and God.

> All Scripture is inspired by God and profitable for teaching, for reproof, for correction, for training in righteousness; that the man of God may be adequate, equipped for every good work (II Tim. 3:16, 17).

God's revelation in Scripture is given to direct us to true knowledge.

The revelation of God in all of creation and in Scripture does not remove the radical Creator-creature distinction. As we will see, God's revelation forms one of the bases upon which that distinction can and must be acknowledged by man (see Fig. 5).

Figure 5

B. The Dependence of Man On God

The Psalmist directs us to remember who we are with these words:

> Know that the Lord Himself is God; It is He who has made us, and not we ourselves (Ps. 100:3).

Man is no less dependent on God than is the rest of creation for he himself was created by God and is sustained by Him. Man is the crown of God's creative activity, but he is still a creature and is returning to dust (Gen. 2:7). "In Him [God] we live and move and exist" (Acts 17:28) and apart from God we are nothing. All that man possesses has been given to him by God. As with the rest of creation, if God were to remove His hand from us, we could not even continue to exist. We exist entirely by the will of God. This total dependence of man on God has many implications, but there are two aspects of our need for God which are especially important for further work in apologetics.

1. Man's Dependent Knowledge

The Creator-creature distinction affects the Christian view of man's ability to know himself, the world around him, and God. In the lessons which follow, we will concern ourselves with man's knowledge in greater detail, especially as it has been affected by sin, but it is important to speak first of man's knowledge in a less specific way. As we have already seen, man is totally dependent on God. This includes his knowledge. God's understanding of Himself and the creation is independent but man's knowledge is dependent. The Psalmist puts it this way:

In thy light we see light (Ps. 36:9).

Apart from God's light of revelation in creation and in Scripture, we can never know light. God knows all and it is upon His knowledge that we must depend if we ourselves are to know. Any true understanding which men have is derived either intentionally or unintentionally from God. This, as we will see, was true of the first man and continues even until now. Jesus Himself claimed:

I am the way, and the *truth*, and the life (John 14:6).

Paul affirmed this, saying that in Christ:

are hidden *all* the treasures of wisdom and knowledge (Col. 2:3).

All that can be properly called truth, not just so-called "religious truth" resides first in God and men know truly only as they come to God's revelation of Himself as the source of truth, for it is God who teaches man knowledge (Ps. 94:10). We will see later that this dependence of man on God in the area of knowledge does not mean that men are without true ability to think and reason nor that they are "programmed" by God in analogy to the way computers "know." Men do actually think, yet, true knowledge is dependent on and derived from God's knowledge as it has been revealed to man.

2. Man's Dependent Morality

As men must depend on God for knowledge in general, they must also depend on Him for direction in the area of morality. In a day when traditional values and goals are being questioned we are forced to ask anew how men are to distinguish between right and wrong, good and bad. The only way to succeed in finding an answer to this and similar questions is once again to affirm the Creator-creature distinction. As the Creator, God has from the beginning been a law-giver who stands above His law, but who expects compliance with it by his creatures. When God said, "It is good," He declared Himself to be the only proper judge between good and evil and He has continued to reserve that right for Himself even until now. To Adam and Eve He said, "from the tree of the knowledge of good and evil you shall not eat" (Gen.2:17). To Moses, He declared, "I am the Lord your God. . . .You shall have no other gods before Me" (Ex. 20:2, 3). Concerning Jesus, God said, "This is my beloved Son with whom I am well pleased; hear Him" (Matt. 17:5). There can be no court to which we take God's judgments; He is the supreme judge. That which He declares concerning morality is binding on all men, and if we wish to know good and evil, we must remember our creaturely dependence on Him in this regard.

Arriving at a biblical approach to apologetics is a difficult task. God is the Creator and if we, His creatures, wish to know truly and choose correctly, we must depend fully on His revelation.

Review Questions:

1. What is significant about the fact that the Bible opens as it does in Genesis 1:1?
2. What do we mean by the "Creator-creature distinction"?
3. How is God independent? Does this mean that He has no contact with the world?
4. How is creation dependent on God? Can you support your answer with Scripture?
5. What are the two basic ways God reveals Himself today? Which of these do we need in order to understand the other properly?

Lesson 3. The Character of Man Before Sin

God created man in His own image, in the image of God He created him; male and female He created them (Gen. 1:27).

An understanding of biblical apologetics rests on a proper view of the character of man. "Know thyself" has been a popular aphorism among thinkers since the early days of philosophy, for a knowledge of ourselves will better equip us for the various tasks which are ours in the world. The Bible looks at the history of the world and mankind in three stages: creation, fall, and redemption. The world was created, it fell under the curse of sin, and it is redeemed by the death and resurrection of Jesus Christ. In line with this threefold perspective, we will examine the character of man in three categories. In this lesson, we will deal with man before the fall, and in the next two lessons, with fallen and redeemed man.

A. Man in the Image of God

In distinction from the rest of creation, man was created in the image of God (cf. Gen 1:27). This fact has far too many implications for us to examine it thoroughly. We shall have to limit ourselves to only a glimpse of the significance of man's creation in God's image. Outwardly, man resembles God in his physical characteristics and abilities. Inwardly, man is able to think and reason as only humans can, and man is uniquely in the image of God because he is a never-perishing soul (cf. Gen. 2:7). Moreover, in further resemblance of his Creator, man was made to rule as king over the earth. As God's representative, he is unearthing the many potentials latent in the creation for use in service to God (cf. Gen. 1:27-31).

While these characteristics are true to some extent of all men in the world, man before the fall was in the image of God in a special way. Before sin, man was the perfect creaturely image of God. Originally,

God made men upright (Eccles. 7:29).

Man was therefore in the image of God without sin. While in the garden of Eden, Adam and Eve lived in harmony with God. They walked before Him without shame. Paul describes this state as possessing:

true knowledge according to the image of the One who created . . . (Col. 3:10).

Elsewhere he says that if one is restored to Adam's original character, he has:

been created in righteousness and holiness of the truth (Eph. 4:24).

From these passages, two important qualities of man before sin can be seen. First, he had "true knowledge" (Col. 3:10). In other words, Adam and Eve never forgot the Creator-creature distinction as it related to their knowledge. They depended on God's revelation of Himself as their source of truth, and they conformed all of their thoughts to the standard of God's revealed truth. It was for this reason that Adam could be given the difficult task of keeping the garden and naming every animal on earth. He was consciously aware of his need to listen to God in every circumstance if he was to have true knowledge. In the same way, before sin, man's knowledge of truth was complemented by his moral character; he possessed the "righteousness and holiness of the truth." Adam knew that by virtue of his creaturehood, he needed to learn from God what was proper and what was not. He and Eve therefore obeyed perfectly all of God's requirements and lived at peace with Him. In every way possible, man before sin knew truth and lived according to that truth (see Fig. 6).

B. Sinless and Finite

Although man was the perfect image of God before sin, he was nevertheless the finite creaturely image of God. God is present everywhere (cf. I Kings 8:27; Isa. 66:1) but man is limited by his physical body to finite existence. God is all-powerful (cf. Ps.

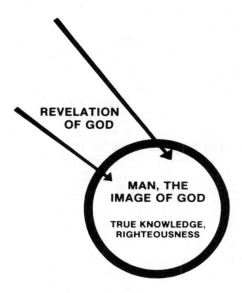

Figure 6

115:3); nothing lies beyond His power. Of course, man, as powerful as his recent technology has made him, is still incomparably weak and limited before God. In the same way, while man's knowledge is limited, God knows all things completely and thoroughly (cf. Job 37:16; Ps. 139:12; Prov. 15:3; Jer. 23:23-24). As the writer of Hebrews has said:

> there is no creature hidden from His sight, but all things are open and laid bare to the eyes of Him with whom we have to do (Heb. 4:13).

Even Adam would have agreed with Isaiah, who said:

> As the heavens are higher than the earth, so are My [God's] ways higher than your ways, and My thoughts than your thoughts (Isa. 55:9).

Indeed, in comparison with God's knowledge, man's thoughts "are mere breath" (Ps. 94:11). Consequently, man is limited to understanding that which is revealed by God and must be satisfied with incomplete knowledge.

> The secret things belong to the Lord our God, but the things revealed belong to us and to our sons forever, that we may observe all the words of this law (Deut. 29:29).

The finiteness of man's knowledge brings us to an important

matter in need of further discussion. Although Adam did not know everything, he still had true knowledge (cf. Col. 3:10). Man's understanding of everything he knows is limited by his perspective, by time, and by the changes occurring in the things he knows. These and other limitations are simply a part of the created order. Yet, we must keep in mind that before the fall into sin, what knowledge Adam did have was derived from God by dependence on His revelation. So, all that Adam knew, he knew truly, for he went to the one source of truth—God. It is plain then that man's finiteness does not make him unable to know truth. As long as knowledge is from God, it is true.

Because he was limited, Adam was faced with mystery, "secret things" (Deut. 29:29) which he could not know. Even the perfect man was unable to put every aspect of his knowledge together in a neatly closed package; there were necessarily loose ends in his thinking, humanly unsolvable difficulties and paradoxes. As great as these mysteries may have been, man's knowledge was not thereby disqualified nor was certainty ruled out. Adam's certainty rested on the revelation of God, not on his own ability to know apart from God. God's complete knowledge of all things validates our incomplete knowledge so long as we depend on Him. Let us take an example of this sort of mystery which confronts us today. The incarnation of our Savior Jesus Christ is full of mysteries. We confess that He is *both* God and man. We can understand His true divinity and His true humanity to some extent, but as we investigate further the implications of the teaching, we arrive at the end of our ability to understand. Can we explain how Jesus "was increasing in wisdom" (Luke 2:52) if He is the all-knowing God? Can we explain how Jesus, who is God, actually died on a cross? We can make some feeble attempts at answering these questions, but any honest person soon realizes that these and other questions are beyond his ability to understand. Although we cannot grasp all of these notions, we can nevertheless be sure that Jesus is both God and man, that He grew in wisdom and that He died. It matters not that we are unable to fully comprehend. Our certainty does not rest on that basis; it rests on the revelation of God.

As we understand more and more Christian truth, we will find that at the end of every doctrine of Scripture there is an inability on the part of man to comprehend the ideas and their relation to other true concepts. There are many seeming contradictions within Christian truth, but this should not cause us to doubt the teaching of the Bible for two reasons. First, it should serve to make us aware of our finiteness. Men must recognize their creatureliness and say with Paul,

> Oh the depth of the riches both of the wisdom and knowledge of God! How unsearchable are His judgements and unfathomable His ways! (Rom. 11:33).

Second, the Bible is not to be doubted when we cannot fit everything together because behind the revelation of the Bible is the mind of God to which nothing is a mystery and in which even the most irreconcilable ideas to our minds are brought together. There is no mystery to God; He knows all perfectly. Mystery is the limitation of the creature, not the Creator. So long as we depend on Him for knowledge, the greatest mysteries will not keep us from truth (see Fig. 7).

C. Logic, God and Man

An issue which continually arises in the discussion and effecting of biblical apologetics is the role of logic in relation to God and man. In this lesson we will be restricted to a very small portion of the question; other facets will be reserved for further discussion later. Adam was created a thinking and reasoning creature; as such he was distinguished from animals and made to reflect the wisdom of God (cf. II Pet. 2:12; Jude 10). As we have seen, in the garden Adam used his reasoning abilities in dependence on God; he patterned his thinking according to God's instruction. To be sure, Adam used logic, at least in an unsophisticated form, but he used it in submission to God. He never disregarded his dependence on God by thinking his logic was able to give him insight independently. Consequently, Adam's use of his reasoning abilities was always subject to limitation and guidance by the revelation of God. God was always looked to as the foundation and shepherd of truth, for Adam was in the image of God and without sin.

From this role which logical reasoning held in man's life before sin entered the world, several observations can be made. First, reason *per se* is not evil. Because Christianity has suffered so many attacks by those who claim to only be "reasonable" and

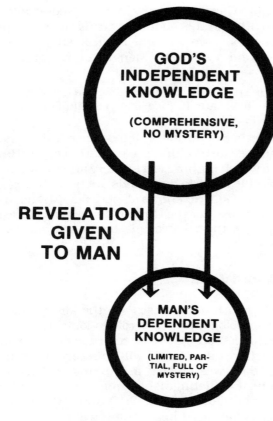

**GOD'S
INDEPENDENT
KNOWLEDGE**

**(COMPREHENSIVE,
NO MYSTERY)**

**REVELATION
GIVEN
TO MAN**

**MAN'S
DEPENDENT
KNOWLEDGE**

**(LIMITED, PAR-
TIAL, FULL OF
MYSTERY)**

Figure 7

"scientific," some Christians have thought their only refuge is to reject reason and science as evil in themselves. Man's use of his mind, however, is not evil, for in the garden Adam reasoned; he used his mind. It was he who named the animals and who kept the garden. To be sure, if human reason is used independently of God, it will lead into falsehood and error, but if it is used in dependence on God's revelation, truth will be discovered. Reason *per se* is not opposed to faith or truth.

Second, logic is not above the Creator-creature distinction. When we speak of human use of reason, we must remember that logic is *at best* merely a reflection of the wisdom and knowledge

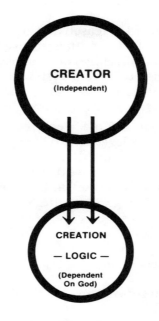

Figure 8

of God. Although in Scripture God does stoop low and reveal Himself in terms of creaturely reason, logic, as we know it, is not above or equal to God, nor is it a part of God's being. Logic, even in its most refined and sophisticated forms, is within the sphere of creation and a quality of man as the image of God, not God Himself.

Because logic is a part of creation, it has limitations. To begin with, logic is a changing and developing system. In fact, there are several systems of logic which are at points in conflict with each other. There is even no definition of "contradiction" that is universally accepted. Besides this, even if all men could agree on one system of reasoning, human logic could not be used as the judge of truth and falsehood. Christianity is at points reasonable and logical but logic meets the end of its ability when it comes to matters like the incarnation of Christ, and the doctrine of the Trinity. Logic is not God and it should never be given the honor due to God alone. Truth is found at the judgment seat of God, not the court of logic.

We must be careful, then, to avoid the two extreme stances

usually taken with regard to reason and logic. Men wish either to reject reason in favor of blind faith or to give logic some amount of independence from God. Neither of these positions is supported by the character of man before sin. Man was created a reasoning creature, but he is expected to realize the limitations of his reason and the dependence of his logic on the Creator (see Fig. 8).

The character of man before sin entered the world is foundational for the task of apologetics. While no one today is entirely without sin, many of the qualities of man before the fall are carried over even to this day. As we defend the Christian faith we deal with men and women descendant from Adam. As such, it is important to have a firm grasp on the state of man before the fall.

Review Questions:

1. In what three categories must we think of the character of man?

2. What does it mean to say that man is in the image of God?

3. Describe Adam's view of his own knowledge and his moral decisions before sin entered the world. Can you support your answer from Scripture?

4. How is man's knowledge limited by his finiteness?

5. Why are there mysteries which men cannot comprehend? Can you give an example of one such mystery?

6. How can we be certain of anything if there are mysteries that we cannot understand?

7. What are two implications concerning the use of logic that we can draw from Adam before the fall?

Lesson 4. The Character of Man in Sin

> But a natural man does not accept the things of the Spirit of God; for they are foolishness to him, and he cannot understand them, because they are Spiritually examined (I Cor. 2:14)

In the preceding lesson we discussed the character of human beings before the fall into sin but our look at man is incomplete if we do not examine the effects of the fall on man. "The knowledge of ourselves lies first in considering what we were given at creation . . . , secondly, to call to mind our miserable condition after Adam's fall."[1] The character of man has changed under the curse of sin. Man is no longer the perfect image of God; he does not live or think as Adam and Eve did before the fall. In fact, as we will see in this lesson, sin has so affected man that he actually denies his total dependence on God. To have an understanding of this condition of man, we will first discuss the original fall of man and then the state of things which followed.

A. The Fall of Mankind

God had made man and woman in His own image and had placed them in the garden of Eden. Since Adam and Eve recognized their creatureliness, they gladly dedicated themselves to the service of God. As time went on, however, man's faithfulness to God was to be tested, for God had placed the tree of the knowledge of good and evil in the middle of the garden and said,

> from the tree of the knowledge of good and evil you shall not eat, for in the day that you eat from it you shall surely die (Gen. 2:17).

[1] John Calvin, *Institutes*, II,1,1.

More was at stake for man than mere abstinence from a particular fruit. "Adam was denied the tree of the knowledge of good and evil to test his obedience and prove that he was willingly under God's command."[2] God had spoken and revealed His will with regard to the forbidden tree. Adam and Eve were put to the test of recognizing or denying the authority of God and their dependence on Him.

The third chapter of Genesis focuses on the fall of man. The serpent, who we discover elsewhere in the Bible was the devil (cf. Gen. 3:15; Rom. 16:20), approached Eve and tempted her to forsake what God had commanded. Placing before the woman the most important choice of her life he said,

> You surely shall not die! For God knows that in the day you eat from it your eyes will be opened, and you will be like God (Gen. 3:4–5).

The serpent's words clearly contradicted God's revelation. Eve was faced with a decision: who was trustworthy? God had said, "you shall die" and the serpent said, "you shall not die." The woman had to believe one or the other. Moreover, the cunning serpent was not satisfied with saying that God was merely in error. He even suggested that if Eve would but eat the fruit the Creator-creature distinction would be removed. "You will be like God," (Gen. 3:5) he boasted.

As foolish as it may seem, Eve was deceived by the lies of the shrewd serpent. The temptation to be like God was too great. Having shaken all reverence for her Creator, Eve decided that she no longer needed to depend on God for true knowledge nor for direction in morality. The serpent had called the reliability of God in these matters into question and Eve had succumbed to his suggestions. Before this time, Eve had accepted God's revelation with a recognition of her total dependence on Him but now she decided that depending on God was optional. A careful reading of Genesis 3:6 shows the essence of Eve's error.

> When the woman saw that the tree was good for food, and that it was a delight to the eyes, and that the tree was desirable to make one wise, she took from its fruit and ate; and she gave also to her husband with her, and he ate.

[2]Ibid., II,1,4.

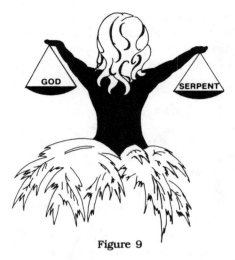

Figure 9

Eve did not immediately reject the Word of God nor did she immediately accept the word of the serpent. Instead, she looked at the tree herself and determined its character by committing herself to independence from God. She said to herself, "Why listen to everyone else? I will make laws for myself; I will decide on my own!" In doing this, Eve rejected the Creator-creature distinction. She took the revelation of the independent God and put it on the same level as the serpent's words and set herself up as the ultimate judge between them (see Fig. 9).

Eve gave the fruit to her husband Adam. He ate and the human race fell under the power of sin. This, then, is the essence of sin; man's rebellion against recognizing his dependence on God in everything and the assumption of his ability to be *independent* of God.

It is important to remember that the Creator-creature distinction continued in effect whether man chose to recognize it or not. Adam and Eve were no less in actual dependence on God after the fall than they were before the fall. They simply refused to acknowledge their dependence. A toddler may deceive himself into thinking he does not need his parents but he is no less a dependent child. In a similar way, Adam and Eve thought they were independent of God, but they still needed God for everything, even the ability to reject Him. God's requirement of Adam and Eve was that they admit their dependence and live according to it. They failed to meet His demand and fell into sin. Thinking themselves to be wise, they became fools, for God's Word was true after all; they died.

B. The Effects of the Fall

The fall of man in the garden was not an isolated event in the past with little effect on man today; the fall brought all men under bondage to sin.

> through one man sin entered into the world, and death through sin, and so death spread to all men because all sinned (Rom. 5:12).

From birth all are corrupted by sin (cf. Ps. 51:5; Eph. 2:3). As Adam and Eve rejected the Creator-creature distinction, all men deny the revelation of God both in all of creation and in His special revelation.

Paul describes the rejection of revelation in all of creation in Romans 1:18–32. There he says that even though creation clearly reveals God's character and His will, unbelieving men suppress or hold back "the truth in unrighteousness" (v. 18). They refuse to acknowledge God as revealed in creation and "their foolish heart was darkened" (v. 21). "Professing to be wise they became fools" (v. 22) for they would worship "the creature rather than the Creator" (v. 25). Because "they did not see fit to have God in knowledge any longer, God gave them over to a depraved mind . . ." (v. 28). Man fallen into sin refuses to acknowledge God's revelation in all aspects of creation.

The unbeliever also fails to give proper place to God's special revelation. Jesus illustrated how Israel asserted her independence of God's special revelation in the parable of the tenant farmers (cf. Matt. 21:33–44). The tenant farmers had their livelihood at the mercy of the landowner but they refused to honor Him. As a result the landowner sent special messengers to the farmers. In fact, He even sent His Son but the farmers hated and killed them all. In the same way, while all should submit to God's special revelation in Scripture, they reject it. In fact, sin has such a firm grip on man that he is actually unable to submit himself to Scripture.

Figure 10

> The mind set on the flesh is hostile toward God; for it does not subject itself to the Law of God, for it is not even able to do so (Rom. 8:7).

Man in his fallen state is, therefore, not capable of understanding God's revelation.

> he cannot understand them, because they are Spiritually examined (I Cor. 2:14).

Instead of bowing to the revelation of God men follow the example of Adam and Eve supposing that all things must be measured "by the yardstick of their own carnal stupidity"[3] (see Fig. 10).

The failure of man to acknowledge God's revelation in nature and to receive the Scriptures as the means for knowing God and His will has left man in a difficult condition. Jeremiah exclaimed in his day,

> Behold, they have rejected the word of the Lord, and what kind of wisdom do they have? (Jer. 8:9).

What can we see if our eyes are closed? What shall quench our thirst if our well is dry? Nothing. The same is true of wisdom and knowledge. God alone "teaches man knowledge" (Ps. 97:4) through His revelation. If we reject His Word, we reject all truth and in principle know nothing but falsehoods.

[3]Ibid., I,2,2.

> The fear of the Lord is the beginning of knowledge (Prov. 1:7).

He who trusts in his own heart (Prov. 28:26) and has no delight in true understanding (Prov. 18:2) is a fool. He hates knowledge (Prov. 1:29) and words of knowledge cannot be found on his lips (Prov. 10:18; 14:7; 19:1). Because of their rejection of God's revelation, men

> walk in the futility of their mind, being darkened in their understanding, excluded from the life of God (Eph. 4:17–18).

For this reason we read,

> The Lord knows the reasonings of the wise, that they are useless (I Cor. 3:20).

So long as men continue to turn away from God's revelation of Himself and His will they will be unable to arrive at true knowledge of themselves, the world, and God.

C. Inconsistencies and Surface Truth

The effects of sin in the life of the non-Christian are fairly obvious when he simply denies the truth revealed in Scripture or grossly misinterprets the world around him. Yet, not all of the thoughts and statements of sinful men are accounted for so simply. How is it that non-Christians can think and express ideas that are correct? Believers and unbelievers both assert that two plus two equals four. Few, if any, would deny that there are words printed on this page. In fact, there are even instances in the Bible where it is acknowledged that fallen men have truth (cf. Matt. 23:1f.; Acts 17:28). How shall we understand these matters in relation to sinful man's rejection of God as the source of truth?

The solution to this problem lies in a closer look at the condition of fallen man and two aspects of his knowledge. First, though unbelievers do reject God's revelation of Himself, they cannot be thoroughly consistent in that rejection. The reason for the inconsistency which is present in every fallen man to some degree is that even sinful men are in the image of God and retain many of man's original abilities (cf. Gen. 9:6; James 3:9). Man still thinks and reasons; he still perceives the world. Because God's common grace restrains the principle of sin and depravity, non-

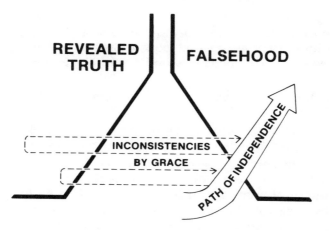

Figure 11

Christians are actually able to think and act according to the remaining effects of their being in God's image without acknowledging Him as their Creator.

> When Gentiles who do not have the Law do by nature the things of the Law . . . they show the work of the Law written in their hearts . . . (Rom. 2:14, 15).

Fallen man begins with the notion of his own independence and ability to know truth apart from God. If he worked this assumption out consistently, he could have no true knowledge for dependence on God is the only way of truth. Even so, the non-Christian can and does fail to be consistent and often turns to his remaining knowledge of God and the world (see Fig. 11). He thereby often thinks and says what we may in some sense call truth.

Along with the inconsistency in the unbeliever's attempts to hold back God's revelation, we can also understand his ability to know truth when we recognize the character of his apprehension of truth. Fallen man's "capacity to understand . . . is an unstable and transitory thing in God's sight. . . ."[4] Non-Christians are able to know truth only by inconsistency with their sinful principles of thought and this fact causes their knowledge to be at best true merely on the surface. An analogy will be helpful. Jesus' words to the Pharisees were often directed toward the

[4]Ibid., I,6,1.

difference between their outward actions and inward motives. The value of their greatest religious tasks was corrupted by their motives of self-righteousness and pride. The Proverbs say that even

the sacrifice of the wicked is an abomination to the Lord (Prov. 15:8).

The Pharisees had outward or surface piety but their godliness was corrupted by what lay behind their outward actions.

The same sort of distinction can be made in the area of knowledge in general. We must never be satisfied with the appearance of seemingly true statements from sinful men. We must be aware of what lies behind the ideas which are presented. For instance, a Jehovah's Witness could honestly say, "Jesus is the Lord." We would all have to agree that his statement is true on the surface. Nevertheless, Jehovah's Witnesses deny the deity of Christ and think of Jesus' Lordship as that of a special angel. So, we would have to consider the statement as false. The reason we can affirm and deny this statement at the same time is found in the difference between the surface statement and that which underlies it. This distinction can be made in terms of what one *says* in contrast with what one *means*, or the assertion *that* something is a fact in contrast with *what* a fact is. One way of discerning this principle is always to ask *what* is meant by *that* which is said or thought. Fallen men may *say that* the world is round but *what* do they *mean* by "world"? Is it the creation of the God of Scripture or the result of a long evolutionary process? They may *say that* honesty is good and murder is bad. Yet, *what* is *meant* by "good and bad"? Are good and bad defined by God's law or some other principle? Like a beautiful tree recently planted in poisonous soil, when non-Christians are inconsistent with their denial of truth and retreat to God's undeniable revelation, the soil of their independence from God pollutes that which is true on the surface. Sometimes, we must go very far beneath the surface before discovering the falsifying meaning, but at the root of every idea and statement which the non-Christian asserts is the assumption "I am independent of God and know this truly on my own apart from Him and the consideration of His will" (see Fig. 12).

To sum up the proper perspective on the true statements made by non-Christians, it may be said that they are true as well as

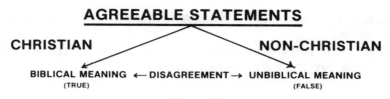

AGREEABLE STATEMENTS

CHRISTIAN   NON-CHRISTIAN

BIBLICAL MEANING ← DISAGREEMENT → UNBIBLICAL MEANING
(TRUE)   (FALSE)

Figure 12

false. Unbelievers may think and speak truth in the sense that their thoughts are sometimes actually from the inescapable revelation of God and are produced by God's common grace through the unavoidable qualities of man as God's image. Moreover, they are true in the sense that the revelation of God may actually confirm the statements on the surface, and by providing an alternate framework for the statements they make, this revelation may lead to the acknowledgement of God and obedience to Him. At the same time, however, we may speak of such statements by unbelievers as false because they are not the result of voluntary obedience to God's revelation but the result of the denial of the Creator-creature distinction. Beyond this, the statements are falsified by the non-Christian framework of meaning and therefore lead away from the worship of God. If nothing else, the mere commitment to human independence falsifies all the non-Christian's statements.

Understanding the condition of man fallen in sin and remaining in unbelief is of vital importance for the defense of Christianity. Recognition of the hopelessness and futility of non-Christian thinking provides direction and gives confidence to the believer defending his faith.

Review Questions:

1. What was the essence of Eve's failure in the garden? How is this sin at the root of every unbeliever's life?

2. How have unbelievers reacted to God's revelation in every aspect of creation? God's special revelation?

3. What effect does commitment to independence have on the knowledge and morality of the unbeliever? Can you support your answer from Scripture?

4. Why are fallen men able to assert truth and perform good deeds?

5. In what sense may non-Christians speak truth? In what sense are their true statements false?

Lesson 5. The Character of Man Redeemed by Christ

> Therefore if any man is in Christ, there is a new creation; the old things passed away; behold, new things have come (II Cor. 5:17).

If it were not for the grace of God, everyone would be lost in sin and under the judgment of God. Yet, God in great mercy sent His divine Son, Jesus Christ, to pay the debt of sin by dying on the cross and to usher in a new age of life by His resurrection. All who have trusted in Him are delivered from the curse of God's wrath and enter into the blessing of God. We have not, therefore, completed our look at man until we consider the character of those redeemed by God in Christ.

A. The Reversal of the Fall

There is a sense in which we may see the application of salvation to an individual's life as the reversal of what occurred by the fall. If you recall, Eve's basic failure was that she assumed her independence from God by refusing to readily submit herself to His Word. Eve rejected the Creator-creature distinction by thinking herself able to know truth by her own insight apart from God. The exact opposite is evident in the life of one who trusts in Christ. Paul makes this plain by saying,

> For since in the wisdom of God the world through its wisdom did not come to know God, God was well-pleased through the foolishness of the message preached to save those who believe (I Cor. 1:21).

Using human wisdom as the criterion for truth, as Eve had done in the garden, leads away from God and into falsehood. So it is that the cross as the way of salvation causes us to turn away from the independence of human and sinful thought in order to know God. Eve thought herself independent and saw herself as ultimate judge. When we truly believe in Christ, we recognize our dependence on the Word of God as uncontestable wisdom and truth. This acceptance of God's Word is the very beginning of redemption in Christ.

> So faith comes by hearing, and hearing by the word of Christ (Rom. 10:17).

The reversal of the fall does not stop with initial conversion. It covers the entirety of the redeeming process. The one who trusts in the message of the gospel is convinced with Paul,

> Let God be found true, though every man be found a liar . . . (Rom. 3:4).

Though the tendency of man in sin is to forsake true knowledge and to falsely assert his independence from God, the believer holds that God's Word can always be trusted for He is true. As Isaiah said,

> I, the Lord, speak righteousness, declaring things that are upright (Isa. 45:19).

God's Word is trustworthy and the believer in Christ confesses his total reliance on it. Despite appearances, despite the advice of others, and despite the temptations of Satan, the believer affirms

> There is no one holy like the Lord, indeed, there is no one besides Thee, nor is there any rock like our God (I Sam. 2:2).

That this attitude toward the Word of God is a reversal of the fall is made clear in the words of Paul to the Corinthians.

> I betrothed you to one husband, that to Christ I might present you as a pure virgin. But I am afraid, lest as the serpent deceived Eve by his craftiness, your minds should be led astray from the simplicity and purity of devotion to Christ (II Cor. 11:2-3).

In this passage Paul is warning the Corinthians against turning away from his preaching of God's Word for they were to be faithful to Christ alone. He warned them in this way because he was afraid that they would fall prey to the same deception which the serpent used in the temptation of Eve. He feared they would turn away from "the simplicity and purity of devotion to Christ" (II Cor. 11:3). Before the fall, Eve listened to God's Word with singularity of devotion. At the fall she turned from God's Word. As

Figure 13

Christians, however, we are to continually receive the Word of Christ with unquestioning devotion. We are to do the very opposite of what Eve did when she sinned. To be redeemed by Christ is to experience the reversal of the fall (see Fig. 13).

B. Restoration by Regeneration

When we think of salvation in Christ we usually think only of the effect that trusting Him will have on our eternal destiny. This end is important, to be sure, but we will at this time focus more carefully on the significance of the reversal of the fall as it affects the character of man in the areas of knowledge and morality. Jesus told Nicodemus the requirement for entering God's kingdom saying,

> You must be born from above (John 3:7).

A new birth must come over the unbeliever. As he was born in Adam and thereby fell in bondage to sin, a new beginning, a regeneration, must occur. Paul put it in these terms.

> Therefore if any man is in Christ, there is a new creation; the old things passed away; behold new things have come (II Cor. 5:17).

When we are saved from our sins we are not only regenerated personally; there is an entirely new sphere of existence (new creation) into which we enter. Therefore the whole life of the believer is to experience the change of regeneration.

Paul's use of the term "new creation" is quite instructive for it points to the relation of redemption and the original state of creation before the fall. When the world and man were first created they were not affected by sin. Yet, because man chose to think himself independent of God the whole creation was cast into sin. In many respects, however, the redeeming work of Christ is the restoration of men and the world back to the original state in which they were first created.

> . . . and put on the new man, which in the likeness of God has been created in righteousness and holiness of the truth (Eph. 4:24).

> . . . put on the new man who is being renewed to a true knowledge according to the image of the One who created him (Col. 3:10).

Believers in Christ are being restored according to the original character of the image of God. They are given righteousness, holiness, and true knowledge, all of which were lost in the fall. Special notice must be given to the fact that restoration by regeneration does not include merely some portion of man. It involves his whole character, even his thinking processes.

> . . . we are taking every thought captive to the obedience of Christ (II Cor. 10:5).

Christians are actually restored to some degree to the original state of man before the fall in every aspect of their personality. We are not merely saved to be in the sweet by and by. We are brought into a new creation and restored as the image of God by regeneration.

As the restored image of God, redeemed man seeks to do justice to God's revelation in all of creation and in Scripture. He realizes that it is not enough to know that rain is the condensation of evaporated water. He asks *what* rain is and how it reveals the character and the will of God. If there were no sin, this would be no problem. Man could simply observe the world and know God through it. Yet, because of sin "it is needful that another and better help be added to direct us aught to the very Creator of the universe."[1] That better help is Scripture. The Christian is committed to searching the Scriptures for the truths leading to the knowledge of salvation and also those truths leading to the

[1]John Calvin, *Institutes*, I,6,1.

knowledge of creation as it reveals God and His will to man. This is not to say that the Bible becomes a textbook of natural science, as if the Christian did not need to look at the world and could merely read his Bible and arrive at scientific truth. Instead, the Scriptures lay down general principles on which every investigation of the world must rest. The true knowledge of rain, for instance, reveals to us the mercy of God and how God expects us to treat enemies with kindness (Matt. 5:45f.). Of course, scientific investigation into the nature of rain will intensify and clarify the Christian's understanding of these things but true knowledge of rain is discovered by investigation resting on and governed by the Scriptures. As a restored creature, the Christian seeks to maintain the Creator-creature distinction in his knowledge and morality and thereby gives proper place to the revelation of God.

C. The Believer and Remaining Sin

The life of the Christian is not without fault. Though he has been restored to the original state, this restoration is not complete until the second advent of Christ. The Christian is involved in a raging battle between righteousness and sin. Paul describes this conflict in these terms.

> For the flesh sets its desire against the Spirit, and the Spirit against the flesh; for these are in opposition to one another, so that you may not do the things that you please (Gal. 5:17).

The Holy Spirit dwelling within the believer is at war with the apostasy of fleshly thought. As a result, there are two principles at work in the believer, one toward obedience and the other toward disobedience. Though the Christian seeks to be dependent on God by looking to His revelation for knowledge and morality, he fails to carry out that desire consistently. At times even the Christian regresses back to the sin of the fall by rebelling against or ignoring the Creator-creature distinction. This regression shows itself in the refusal to acknowledge the revelation of God in all things, including the Scriptures. As the non-Christian cannot escape his qualities as God's image, the Christian cannot escape fully the remains of sin in his life. He is inconsistent with his principle of total dependence on God and

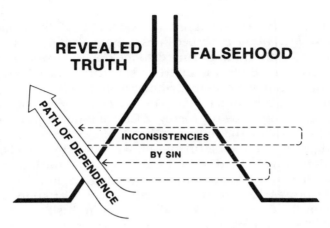

REVEALED TRUTH　　**FALSEHOOD**

INCONSISTENCIES

BY SIN

PATH OF DEPENDENCE

Figure 14

thereby maintains falsehoods in his thoughts and actions (see Fig. 14).

It is for this reason that the Christian is repeatedly encouraged to avoid and resist sin. Paul says,

> Even so consider yourselves to be dead to sin, but alive to God in Christ Jesus. Do not let sin reign in your mortal body that you should obey its lusts (Rom. 6:11, 12).

and in a more positive fashion,

> Do not be conformed to this world, but be transformed by the renewing of your mind (Rom. 12:2).

Dependence on God for knowledge and morality does not come automatically even for the Christian. It must involve determined effort, seeking after "sanctification without which no one will see the Lord" (Heb. 12:14). It is a long and difficult task but one which must be continually furthered if we are to know God and His will. As we think of the Christian's ability to know truly because of regeneration and the reversal of the fall, we must also remember that sin still affects the Christian life.

The character of man redeemed by Christ is basic to an understanding of biblical apologetics. The work of Christ on the cross and in His resurrection has renewed to true knowledge and righteousness those who believe in Him. Though sin is still present, the one who is redeemed by Christ can depend on God for knowledge and morality.

Review Questions:

1. How is regeneration a reversal of the fall?
2. In what sense is redeemed man restored to the state of man before the fall?
3. How does the reversal and restoration experienced by the believer cause him to deal with the revelation of God in all things and in Scripture?
4. How does remaining sin affect the believer's knowledge and morality?

Lesson 6. The Non-Christian Point of View

> See to it that no one takes you captive through philosophy and empty deception, according to the tradition of men, according to the elementary principles of the world, rather than according to Christ (Col. 2:8).

From our brief look at the character of man, it is evident that there are two kinds of people living in the world today, holding opposite views of God, the world, and themselves. These two perspectives will be called Christian and non-Christian philosophy for they are rooted in either the commitment to total dependence on God or the allegiance to independence. Moreover, these perspectives involve more than so-called "religious matters" and "theological issues"; they permeate every aspect of the lives of those involved. We will summarize the basic views of non-Christian philosophy and will give attention to Christian philosophy in the next lesson.

A. The Structure

The peculiarities of non-Christian philosophy are a result of the character of non-Christians. In Ephesians 4:17–19 Paul describes non-Christians in such a way as to reveal the sort of philosophy they are capable of producing. They walk

> . . . in the futility of their mind, being darkened in their understanding, excluded from the life of God, because of the ignorance that is in them, because of the hardness of their heart; and they having become callous, have given themselves over to sensuality, for the practice of every kind of impurity with greediness.

Non-Christians still remain under the curse of sin; denying the Creator-creature distinction and committing themselves to independence from God, they live in futility. All their efforts are darkened and impure. It is for this reason that Paul elsewhere describes non-Christian philosophy in these terms:

> See to it that no one takes you captive through philosophy and empty deception . . . (Col. 2:8).

Care must be taken to understand Paul correctly. He is not opposed to philosophy in general; he himself was a sort of a philosopher. He is, instead, opposed to non-Christian philosophy. Philosophy based on allegiance to independence claims truth but offers nothing except ruin and eternal death. Consequently, Paul speaks of non-Christian philosophy as "empty deception." Many are deceived by the views of those without Christ, but they will one day discover the emptiness which is truly there. There have been many important unbelievers who have made worthwhile contributions to man's knowledge and life, but as a whole non-Christian philosophy has the potential of nothing more than empty deception.

We may think at first that Paul may have overstated the case, but his words which follow prove otherwise.

> . . . empty deception, according to the tradition of men, according to the elementary principles of the world rather than according to Christ (Col. 2:8).

In spite of the value which may be found in various portions of non-Christian thought the one thing which empties it and makes it deceptive is that commitment common to all non-Christians: philosophy must be based on human independence. Non-Christian philosophy is not neutrally based. It rests on loyalty to the "tradition of men" and "the elementary principles of the world." Nothing can be true unless it is shown to be so by independent human thought. To be even more pointed, Paul indicates the truly religious character of this allegiance, saying that non-Christian philosophy is according to man *"rather than Christ."* In other words, all non-Christians reject the claims of Christ in their determination to be independent. Even those who seek to be neutral deny Christ's claim as the unquestioned Lord of the universe. To say that Christianity *may be true* is to say it may not be true.

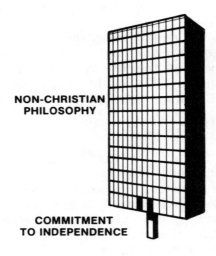

NON-CHRISTIAN PHILOSOPHY

COMMITMENT TO INDEPENDENCE

Figure 15

But God demands complete loyalty to His Word. In these few words, Paul has penetrated to the very heart of non-Christian philosophy. Apart from unintended inconsistencies, non-Christians never think nor act according to any principle other than their own supposed independence. It is only after the unbeliever is called of God and regenerated that he may do otherwise. In this sense, non-Christian philosophy may be compared to a large building which rests entirely on the one supporting beam of allegiance to independence (see Fig. 15).

Commitment to independence is so fundamental to non-Christian philosophy that no matter how much the unbeliever may claim otherwise, every reason he may give to support his commitment is actually *resting on* it. If a non-Christian is challenged to give a reason for his religious commitment he may respond in a number of ways, but he will always respond with a reason that is supposedly valid according to his principle of independence. He may argue that his experience has in some way informed him of his independence, but his trust in experience as a criterion for truth is itself founded on that allegiance. Essentially, non-Christians try to lift themselves by their own boot-straps, supporting their commitment to independence by arguments founded on their commitment to independence. Non-Christian philosophy may therefore be compared to a building whose roof upholds its foundation; there is no solid ground

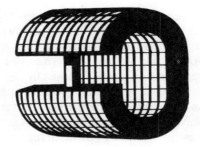

Figure 16

beneath it (see Fig. 16). Non-Christian philosophy is indeed "according to the tradition of men."

B. The Dilemma

When man rejected the Creator-creature distinction and committed himself to independence from God, he ruled out all possibility of acquiring true knowledge. Man was thrown into a dilemma which cannot be avoided by the unbeliever and which reveals the futility of sinful thinking. In analogy to the ancient Greek theatre where the same actor would often play several roles by changing masks, the spiritually blind, deaf, and dumb unbeliever insists on wearing two masks. When turning from God, the unbeliever asserts with *absolute certainty* that the biblical distinction between the Creator and His creature is false; he therefore puts on the mask of *absolute certainty.* Yet, when turning from God, the unbeliever is left in the postion of having no solid ground for knowledge and must therefore wear the mask of *total uncertainty.* While an unbeliever may wear one or the other mask at different times, beneath the mask he may wear the unbeliever is caught in the unsolvable dilemma of being both absolutely certain and totally uncertain at the same time. This unmasking of non-Christian claims and the exposure of this dilemma becomes an important part of a biblical defense of Christianity. Consequently, we shall look at this dilemma of non-Christian thought in some detail.

On the one hand, if the unbeliever claims to have absolute certainty, he can do so only by ignoring his total uncertainty. As illustrated before, certainty is impossible for the non-Christian since he has rejected the only source of true knowledge and is left to finite speculation. For the unbeliever to hold to any view tenaciously, he must do so in total disregard of his limited awareness and his rebellion against God. On the other hand, if the unbeliever claims total uncertainty, questioning man's ability to know, he does so only by ignoring that his view is in reality a statement of absolute certainty. Often this position is presented by the unbeliever as an attempt to avoid arrogance and dogmatism. He may say that we cannot be sure of what we think we know or that we may arrive only at "probable knowledge." Such a stance may seem less presumptuous on the surface, but it is actually a statement of absolute certainty as well as total uncertainty. Non-Christians who claim total uncertainty for man's knowledge say, "It is *absolutely certain* that there are no absolute certainties." The unbeliever can continue to hold this view only as he ignores how absolutely certain he must be to hold it.

It would be helpful at this point to illustrate further how non-Christian philosophy exhibits the dilemma of simultaneously holding to absolute certainty and total uncertainty. We shall do so by considering three major concerns of human thought: God, the external world, and man himself. This description is far from exhaustive for we shall give only a few examples for the sake of illustration. These matters are, nevertheless, very important for a biblical apologetic and will be discussed further in the lessons which follow.

1. Regarding God

One way in which the futility of non-Christian philosophy can be seen regards the question of God's existence. On the one hand, the unbeliever may be an atheist, holding that it is *absolutely certain* that there is no God. In holding this view, however, the unbeliever attempts to ignore the fact that his limited investigation of the universe and beyond compels him on his own ground to be *totally uncertain* about God's existence. Since the unbeliever has not examined all the possible evidence for God's existence, he cannot be *absolutely certain* that He does not exist. This does not mean, however, that the unbeliever may safely claim that God's existence is uncertain. In taking this stance of agnosticism, he is thrown into the same dilemma as the atheist. The unbeliever holds this view of *total uncertainty* while ignoring that agnosticism necessarily involves the *absolute certainty* that God has not made Himself known in such a way as to demand recognition and submission from all men. The agnostic is absolutely certain that God's existence is uncertain. As a result, the unbeliever cannot deny, or claim ignorance of, the existence of God without exhibiting the futility of his rebellion against God.

2. Regarding the External World

The dilemma of unbelieving philosophy shows itself in what non-Christians have to say about their created environment as well. The claim of *absolute certainty* is made, for instance, when the non-Christian says that the world is in some sense orderly and understandable. He is absolutely certain that the order he discerns is in reality actually there. Yet, the non-Christian is faced with the fact that he has not investigated and cannot investigate the entire external world in such a way as to avoid *total uncertainty*. The presence of the unknown calls into question all that the unbeliever claims to know. *Total uncertainty* regarding the external world often involves the notion that the world does not have order and is ruled by chance and makes no sense to man. It is obvious that even when the unbeliever denies the possibility of knowing the world in this fashion, he is making a statement of *absolute certainty* about the character of the world. He knows for certain that the world is of such a character that it is unordered and that it is a product of mere chance. Once again, the unbeliever is faced with the dilemma of being absolutely certain and totally uncertain at the same time.

3. Regarding Man

It is not terribly surprising that unbelievers show the futility of their thought when considering God and the external world. Yet, it must be seen that non-Christians are unable to escape this problem even when they speak with respect to themselves. The position of *absolute certainty* is taken whenever non-Christians attempt to describe man. In one way or another unbelievers pervert the biblical picture of man as the image of God and substitute their own conception of man apart from dependence on God. Man may be thought of as a god or as a mere animal. He may be thought of as important or unimportant. Whatever the case, the unbeliever making such a claim of *absolute certainty* ignores the fact that his limited investigation of the nature of man returns him to *total uncertainty*. On the other hand, some unbelievers may be convinced that man cannot be sure of who he is. Yet, his *total uncertainty* is a statement of *absolute certainty* that man's true character cannot be known for sure. Even the unbeliever's thoughts concerning the nature of his own existence leave him in the dilemma of all rebellious thought against God.

No matter what he may claim or profess, the unbeliever is inevitably absolutely certain and totally uncertain. Consequently, he is left unable to say anything about God, the world, or man— even that he is uncertain about them. Non-Christian philosophy is based on commitment to independence and that commitment has brought man into futility and hopelessness.

In apologetics, we deal with unbelievers and their way of thinking. It is therefore important to know the character of their point of view. The structure and dilemma of unbelieving thought described here is not comprehensive, but those elements which have been covered are true of all non-Christian thinking and should be understood by the Christian apologist.

Review Questions:

1. How is it that all of non-Christian philosophy is founded on the unbeliever's commitment to independence?
2. Why is commitment to independence unable to be supported?
3. What is the dilemma which all non-Christians face?
4. Illustrate the dilemma of non-Christian thought with regard to God, the world, and man.

Lesson 7. The Christian Point of View

See to it that no one takes you captive through philosophy and empty deception, according to the tradition of men, according to the elementary principles of the world, rather than according to Christ (Col. 2:8).

In the last lesson we examined the basic structure and the inescapable dilemma of the non-Christian point of view. In this lesson we will be concerned with contrasting Christian philosophy with non-Christian philosophy. This shall be done first by setting forth the character of Christian philosophy and second by discussing the relationship existing between the two points of view.

A. The Structure

Unlike non-Christians, believers in Christ are capable of much more than darkened futility. As the apostle Paul said,

Now we have received, not the spirit of the world, but the Spirit who is from God, that we might know the things freely given to us by God (I Cor. 2:12).

Christians are able to know and follow the truth of God's revelation and therefore produce a philosophy which is not according to independent human perspectives. Believers are actually able to develop a philosophy pleasing to God. The reason for this lies in the religious commitment at the base of the Christian point of view. After describing non-Christian philosophy as we have seen in Colossians 2:8, Paul goes on to reveal the nature of the religious commitment which is fundamental to Christian philosophy.

> For in Him [Christ] all the fulness of Deity dwells in bodily form, and in Him you have been made complete, and He is head over all rule and authority . . . (Col. 2:9-10).

In these verses Paul gives reasons for having Christian philosophy which is according to Christ. He gives three important ideas in this regard. First, "in Him all the fulness of Deity dwells." Christ is God in bodily form and philosophy should be based on commitment to Him and His Word revealed in Scripture. God alone knows the universe exhaustively; He alone can teach truth to man. So, since Christ is God we must commit ourselves to Him if we are to have a view which is more than empty deception. Second, "in Him you have been made complete." It is only by union with Christ by faith that we are made able to see God, the world and ourselves correctly. Apart from faith in Him as the fundamental commitment of our lives we can have no true philosophy. The third reason Paul gives for having philosophy according to Christ is that "He is head over all rule and authority." To trust any principle as more basic than total dependence on God is to suppose that there is another authority over Christ. Yet, there is no court to which we may take Christ. There is no judge over Him. Therefore, what He declares must be accepted without a question for He is the absolute authority in all things. Every aspect of Christian philosophy should rest on the one commitment to dependence on God. Christian philosophy may be compared to a large building which is supported by the one beam of allegiance to dependence on Christ (see Fig. 17).

The Christian's commitment to dependence on God is often misunderstood in two ways. On the one hand, it is often thought that commitment to Christ involves only church-related matters. So-called secular affairs are not affected by this commitment. This view is, however, mistaken, for loyalty to the principle of dependence extends to all areas of life. Even in farming the believer recognizes that his knowledge is from God.

> Does he not level its surface, and sow dill and scatter cummin and plant wheat in rows, barley in its place, and rye within its area? For his God instructs and teaches him properly (Isa. 28:25-26).

All our wisdom and knowledge comes from God,

> Who teaches us more than the beasts of the earth, and makes us wiser than the birds of heaven (Job 35:11).

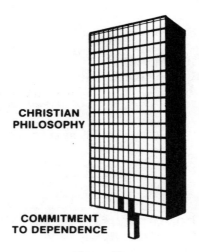

CHRISTIAN
PHILOSOPHY

COMMITMENT
TO DEPENDENCE

Figure 17

The Christian seeks to depend on God in all things so that he may handle all things according to this principle:

> . . . whatever you do in word or deed, do all in the name of the Lord Jesus, giving thanks through Him to God the Father (Col. 3:17).

On the other hand, the commitment of total dependence is sometimes misunderstood to mean that Christian philosophy is merely listening to the Scriptures and praying. Yet, Christians do not get the entirety of their philosophy just from the Bible and prayer, as important as they may be. This passive picture of the Christian enterprise is incorrect. The Christian looks at the world and discovers answers to his questions by active inquiry and investigation. God has not revealed in Scripture detailed answers to every specific question that may be asked. He has, however, given us guidelines within which we are to build our philosophy. When God commanded Noah to build the ark, certain guidelines were set forth by special revelation but the specifics were learned by applying those principles revealed to the situation. For instance, God told Noah to seal the ark but the amount of tar was not specified. Noah therefore had to determine the amount of tar to be used by seeing how much was needed to keep the ark from leaking. Believers are commanded to "subdue the earth and rule . . ." (Gen. 1:28), but detailed directives are not given in Scripture for every aspect of that pursuit. Christian philosophy

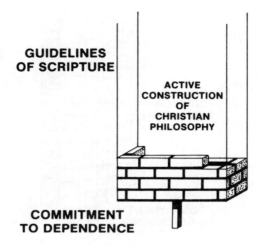

GUIDELINES OF SCRIPTURE

ACTIVE CONSTRUCTION OF CHRISTIAN PHILOSOPHY

COMMITMENT TO DEPENDENCE

Figure 18

is not merely reading the Bible and praying. It is construction regulated by the principles of Scripture (see Fig. 18).

Unlike non-Christians, Christians have solid ground beneath their religious commitment of dependence on God. It is true that if a Christian seeks to justify his dependence by some evidence, that evidence will be itself based on human dependence. For instance, a Christian may argue that his limited mental ability in comparison with the magnitude of the universe is a reason for depending on God. Even so, however, that reason is compelling only if human dependence on God is already accepted. As with non-Christian philosophy, there is circularity also in Christian philosophy. Yet, one important difference remains: the notion of human dependence does not depend on itself for ultimate support. It rests on the solid ground of God and His revelation. When asked why he is dependent on God, the Christian will respond that he is commanded to be so by the revelation of God, and that Scripture is authoritative for the Christian because it is God's Word. He will claim that he knows that the Bible is God's Word by the testimony of the Holy Spirit and the redeeming work of Christ. God, Christ, the Holy Spirit, and Scripture all verify themselves and each other for there can be no authority to which the ultimate authorities appeal. As far as the believer is concerned there is no one greater by whom God may swear to His authority than Himself (see Fig. 19).

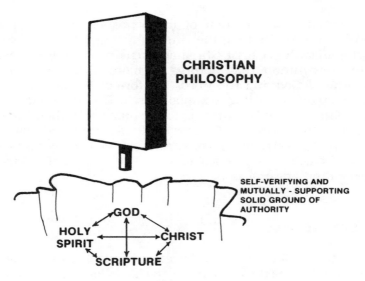

CHRISTIAN
PHILOSOPHY

SELF-VERIFYING AND
MUTUALLY - SUPPORTING
SOLID GROUND OF
AUTHORITY

GOD

HOLY
SPIRIT

CHRIST

SCRIPTURE

Figure 19

A charge that is often brought against the Christian at this point is that his commitment to dependence on God is itself an independent decision. In other words, the non-Christian may claim that underlying dependence on God is the independent process of determining that Christianity is the best choice of religions in the world. To be sure, from a non-Christian perspective this is what seems to have happened. Yet, the Christian realizes this is not the case for he did not commit himself to dependence on God after an independent decision to do so. He was given the grace of God's regeneration apart from his own will. He was thereby *enabled* to commit himself to total dependence.

> So then it does not depend on the man who wills or the man
> who runs, but on God who has mercy (Rom. 9:16).

There is no independent human choice underlying commitment to Christ. The Creator who speaks for Himself and His revelation is alone the ground on which the Christian faith stands.

Both Christians and non-Christians are involved in circularities; they are impossible to avoid when considering our most basic conviction. Yet, an important difference must be seen between them. Non-Christian circularity consists of the attempt to justify the groundless assumption of independence by independent thought and results from the sinner's inability to do otherwise apart from faith in Christ. Christian circularity, however, consists of the recognition that nothing is more ultimate than the authority of God and His Word. The former is the evidence of futile thought struggling to support itself. The latter is the proof of enlightened minds returning to the only one without need of further support, God the Creator of all. Despite the similarities, these differences form a great chasm between the two views of the world which is crossed only by the one touched by the regenerating grace of God.

B. The Answer

Christian philosophy provides escape from the futility of the non-Christian dilemma. In Christ the basis for man's certainity and the answer to his uncertainty is found. Christian philosophy is supported by the commitment to dependence on God which rests on God and His revelation. Because God is seen as the source of all knowledge, the Christian does not face the problem of being irreconcilably certain and uncertain. To be sure, there is certainty and uncertainty in Christian philosophy but these are companions under the Lordship of Christ.

On the one hand, the Christian may be certain of man's knowledge so long as it is dependent on God's revelation. Resting our philosophy on God and His revelation means accepting as certain those things revealed. Unlike the non-Christian, the Christian's certainty is not destroyed by what he does not know. God knows everything exhaustively and is therefore able to provide for man even in the face of his finiteness. So long as man depends on God's revelation for understanding God, the world, and himself, he will know truly without fear of error.

On the other hand, there is uncertainty for the Christian. He recognizes that he is unable to fathom the knowledge of all things. There are matters which are beyond his comprehension and which have not been revealed by God. In such areas the Christian confesses uncertainty and trusts God's wisdom and understanding. For example, the believer is unable to solve the mystery of Christ's divinity and humanity. Nevertheless, he trusts that it is no mystery to God and that it is true because He has said so. Depending on God is trusting Him in those areas in which we cannot have understanding. In this sense, Christians may be said to have *dependent uncertainty*.

In order to make clear the difference between Christian and non-Christian certainty and uncertainty, we shall look at several illustrations of the Christian perspective on these matters. Unbelievers are in the dilemma of absolute certainty and total uncertainty. Christians, however, find the solution to this difficulty by having dependent certainty and dependent uncertainty. We shall show how this solution relates to the Christian concept of God, the world, and man.

1. Regarding God

The Christian has dependent certainty about the existence and the character of God because he receives as true the revelation of God in Scripture. God has spoken and revealed Himself that He might be known by those who commit themselves to belief in His Son. Even so, the Christian has dependent uncertainty because he does not know everything about God. God has kept some things hidden; moreover, the remaining sin in the believer's life keeps him from knowing that which is revealed as he ought. Even so, this uncertainty does not destroy all that Christians do know of God for God has all understanding and knowledge, and Christian philosophy depends on the revelation of the all-knowing God.

2. Regarding the World

Christian philosophy is not caught in the dilemma of non-Christian thought when it considers the external world. Dependent certainty is found in the Christian view because the Scriptures teach that God has created an orderly world that is understandable and that He has provided guidelines in the Bible for understanding. Dependent uncertainty is present in the Christian point of view for several reasons. It takes time to apply the teaching of the Bible to the many aspects of the whole universe. Moreover, the presence of sin brings in the possibility that the Christian may neglect the Bible or misunderstand the world, the Bible, or both. Consequently, Christian philosophy has dependent certainty and dependent uncertainty when considering the external world.

3. Regarding Man

When considering himself, the Christian is dependently certain and uncertain once again. The Christian knows that he is the image of God because God has revealed it in Scripture. Yet, as there are unknown aspects of the external world, there are mysteries about ourselves that the Christian is unable to understand. Moreover, sin causes the believer to misunderstand and sometimes reject the truth of his own character. Even so, the Christian is committed to the notion that God understands fully the character of man. So, while the Christian is dependently uncertain, he is dependently certain as well.

While non-Christians have severed their relationship with God and have therefore fallen prey to the dilemma of God's judgment, Christians have been reunited to God and have found in Him the confidence needed for certainty and the solution to their uncertainty.

C. The Myth of Neutrality

Now that we have seen the difference between Christian and non-Christian philosophy, it is important to see that these points of view are the only positions which can be taken by man. To be sure, both Christians and non-Christians may be more or less consistent with their perspectives, but there is no area of neutrality between the two philosophies. In contrast to the biblical perspective, some Christians and non-Christians fail to recognize that there is no stance of neutrality, a place to stand outside allegiance to independence or dependence. Not all unbelievers claim neutrality for some are openly committed to their religious beliefs. Nevertheless, especially in the framework of twentieth century appreciation for science, many non-Christians claim that they have no fundamental allegiance or at least arrived at their convictions after looking at the world from a neutral standpoint. Hardly a day goes by when we do not hear someone say, "I just want to deal with the objective facts as they really are. I want to keep away from religious questions." As well meaning as they may be, these non-Christians are far from being neutral. They simply fail to realize that even seeking neutrality is a rejection of Christ. He does not ask for "neutral honesty" for such a stance is just a disguised form of allegiance to independence. As Jesus said,

> He who is not with Me is against Me; and he who does not gather with Me scatters (Matt. 12:30).

As odd as it may seem, there is also a sense in which Christians often try to find a place of neutrality. In fact, the idea of an area of neutrality between the Christian and non-Christian has been a central idea to much of apologetics in the past. Essentially, Christians sometimes wrongly seek a common ground between the believer and the unbeliever upon which they may construct a case for the credibility of Christianity. It is important for the development of a biblical apologetic to look at some of these supposed neutral ideas and see why they are not neutral at all.

Logical consistency is offered as a principle upon which believers and unbelievers agree. If we want to show the non-Christian that Christianity is true we may present the logic of belief in God, Christ, and Scripture and thereby reason him, if not into the kingdom, at least in that direction. Yet, care must be taken, for while Christians and non-Christians may agree on the necessity of well-ordered thought, the Christian concept of the limits and functions of logic differs greatly from that of unbelievers. Human reason, in its purest and most sophisticated form is nevertheless creaturely and influenced by the allegiance of the one reasoning. Logic is not neutral.

Sometimes sense experience is suggested as a sphere of neutrality. It is supposed that the non-Christian sees and hears the same things the Christian does and that there is therefore a neutral ground on which to operate. Even so, we must remember that while both may be exposed to the same information, Christians are committed to understanding that information as it really is in light of God's revelation, and non-Christians are committed to misconstruing the world in terms of their allegiance to independence. In fact, there are no so-called facts of any science that believers and unbelievers hold in common. Whether in psychology, biology, history, mathematics, philosophy, theology, etc., the facts of the science are understood differently by Christians and non-Christians so that they are not neutral. There is no neutral ground for talking about "facts" without the influence of our fundamental commitments. We either understand the facts as Christians or we understand them as non-Christians.

An objection sometimes raised against this notion is the question, How can Christians communicate effectively with non-Christians? The answer to this question lies in the fact that while there is no neutrality and no point of actual agreement between believers and unbelievers, we do have in common the world we live in, our creation in the image of God and the free offer of the gospel. Christians and non-Christians both live in the same world. We walk down the same sidewalks, shop in the same stores and eat the same food. In this sense we are able to perform the same mechanical functions in this world. As the image of God, even fallen man reasons, thinks, senses things, and is able to use human language. Consequently, we are able to communicate and actually come to surface agreements, while our radical differences remain. Moreover, as the image of God, the non-Christian knows God and His demands in his heart. Though he denies it, every fact of creation speaks to him of God. Even the very words of the Christian speak to the awareness of God which never fully escapes him. Finally, we may communicate effectively with the non-Christians because the potential of the regenerating work of the Holy Spirit is always present. It is by the gospel spoken to deaf ears that the Holy Spirit opens the heart and brings about faith in Christ. The recognition of the mythical nature of neutrality does not destroy all hope for effective communication with the unbeliever. In fact, it is only when we recognize that there is no neutrality that we begin to communicate with the non-Christian in a way that is relevant to his need for Christ.

There are two opposing views existing in the world today. Without a recognition of these perspectives a biblical apologetic cannot be developed.

Review Questions:

1. What is the fundamental commitment of Christian philosophy?

2. How should Christians seek to justify their commitment?

3. Why is it important to appeal to God and Scripture as the solid ground under our commitment?

4. How does Christian circularity differ from non-Christian circularity?

5. What is the Christian solution to the dilemma of non-Christian thought?

6. Why are dependent certainty and uncertainty complementary in the Christian system?

7. How do non-Christians and Christians sometimes claim neutrality?

8. If there is no neutral ground, how can believers communicate effectively with unbelievers?

Lesson 8. Attitudes and Actions

> . . . give an account for the hope that is in you, yet with gentleness and reverence; and keep a good conscience so that in the thing in which you are slandered, those who revile your good behavior in Christ may be put to shame (I Pet. 3:15-16).

Now that we have looked at some aspects of the biblical teaching about men and their philosophies, we may turn our attention to matters which relate more directly to the practice of apologetics. Those ideas which have been covered thus far are significant as a background for defending the faith but a great deal more needs to be said about the "how to's" of biblical apologetics. In this lesson we will concern ourselves with some of the basic attitudes and actions important to defending the faith.

In an earlier lesson we saw that I Peter 3:15 set forth the responsibility of every Christian to prepare a defense of the gospel. A closer look at the passage reveals that we are not only instructed to give an apology but there are also valuable directives for *how* to make a defense. Peter deals with the attitudes and actions of apologetics by first focusing on the need for a biblical *method* saying, "Sanctify Christ as Lord" (3:15). Second, he refers to the attitudes of "gentleness and reverence" (3:15) when *approaching* the non-Christian. Third, he deals with the importance of "a good conscience" and "good *behavior* in Christ" (3:16). Following these basic categories, though reversing the order, we find that the Scriptures have a great deal to say about the relation of apologetics to our lives, our approach, and our methods.

A. A Consistent Life

A consistent daily Christian walk is an indispensable aspect of a biblical apology. All too often Christians become so interested

in the techniques of practicing apologetics or the theory supporting apologetics that they forget how their lives affect their
defense. It is this neglect which often reduces Christian apologetics
to hot air, empty words without the concrete testimony of a godly
life. Knowing these things, Peter warns his readers to live with a
"good conscience" in such a way that they may be reviled only for
"good behavior in Christ" (I Pet. 3:16). The non-Christian world
often judges the value of the gospel by the consistency of life
observable in the believer. At church, work, or at home, we render
our defense ineffectual by inconsistencies in our lives. On occasion
one can hear a Christian defending the faith before an unbeliever
and at the same time attacking his Christian brethren with
whom he has differences on secondary matters. Such Christians
often fail to realize that their outspoken opposition to other
believers actually hinders their defense of the faith. In fact, there
is hardly a greater obstacle to Christian apologetics than the
fighting and bickering which goes on in the church. Jesus
showed his concern about the affect of disunity on the church's
testimony to the world by saying,

> I in them, and Thou in Me, that they may be perfected in unity,
> that the world may know that Thou didst send Me . . . (John
> 17:23).

We must fill our churches with Christian love and unity if we are
to be convincing to a world of disbelief. One factor which often
hinders the Christian from defending the faith at work or school
is his own failure to be blameless before his peers and superiors.
An employee who becomes intoxicated at the company Christmas
party can hardly stand with boldness for the gospel when "the
real meaning of Christmas" is discussed the next Monday morning.
A Christian student will find it difficult to defend Christianity
before his class, if the night before he was caught cheating on his
assignments. In our neighborhoods, the unity of our homes, the
physical appearance of our houses, our friendly and helpful
attitudes toward our neighbors all affect our ability to offer an
effective defense of the faith. When these areas of our lives fall
short of the biblical standard our apology will fall short as well.
Christ's name will be disgraced and He will be the object of
slander and mockery on our account.

Even the more private areas of our Christian lives strengthen
or weaken our defense of Christianity. The basic practices of

daily Bible reading, meditation and prayer are vital to a biblical apology. According to Psalm 1, the righteous man is one whose

> delight is in the law of the Lord, and in His law he meditates day and night (Ps. 1:2).

We must involve ourselves daily in the reading and application of God's Word to our lives. Otherwise we will wander from the paths of righteousness and make our defense words of hypocrisy. Moreover, as we will see, central to a biblical method of defending the faith is the ability to answer the objections of non-Christians with biblical answers. Only one who is familiar with the Bible through regular reading and meditation will have the wealth of knowledge necessary to give biblical answers to the questions of non-Christians. Without the knowledge of Scripture a biblical defense is practically impossible.

Moreover, a consistent prayer life is a key to effective apologetics. Christianity is not a religion of impersonal assent to certain religious notions, defensible by rigid arguments. It is the dynamic personal relationship of the believer with God through Christ. It is in prayer that we call God, "Our Father in heaven." A life of prayer is one drawn close to God and aware of the living power of His Holy Spirit. Paul said,

> pray without ceasing (I Thess. 5:17).

It is only as our lives are full of prayer that we shall see the development of a biblical apologetics in our lives. This is especially true in the actual practice of defending the faith. Too often, Christians study apologetics and gain confidence in themselves. This self-confidence exhibits itself in that they approach the non-Christian without the slightest acknowledgment of their need for God's help in the situation. Though they may be confident and work hard at defending the faith, it is seldom that such Christians see much fruit from their labor. They may confound the unbeliever but they will not convert him by their own power. We must be consistent in prayer before we approach our opponents and after we have spoken with them that we may be confident in Christ alone.

The need for a consistent Christian walk cannot be too greatly emphasized. Without it, our efforts in apologetics are in vain. We may try to talk non-Christians into heaven but if we live as those destined for hell, we can hardly hope for much success. The

mightiest defenders of the faith will fall if they lack a consistent
life.

B. A Careful Approach

In I Peter 3:15, 16 Peter speaks of the manner of approach we
should have in biblical apologetics saying that we should do so
"with gentleness and reverence." Peter reminds us that we must
be careful when speaking to the non-Christian; our approach can
make all the difference in the world when defending the faith. In
fact, sometimes an approach speaks louder than the actual
words. There are numerous examples of non-Christians who
were not persuaded by the arguments but by the attitudes of the
apologist speaking to them. There are many passages of Scripture
which give direction for our approach. We shall look at a few of
these and then summarize their teaching.

> Conduct yourselves with wisdom toward outsiders, making the
> most of the opportunity. Let your speech always be with grace,
> seasoned as it were, with salt, so that you may know how you
> should respond to each person (Col. 4:5-6).

> Remind them to be subject to rulers, to authorities, to be
> obedient, to be ready for every good deed, to malign no one, to be
> uncontentious, gentle, showing every consideration for all men
> (Titus 3:1-2).

> But refuse foolish and ignorant speculations, knowing they
> produce quarrels. And the Lord's bond-servant must not be
> quarrelsome, but be kind to all, able to teach, patient when
> wronged, with gentleness correcting those who are in opposition,
> if perhaps God may grant them repentance leading to the
> knowledge of the truth, and they may come to their senses and
> escape from the snare of the devil (II Tim. 2:23-26).

To be sure, these verses are only a few of the portions of Scripture
which could be related to a proper approach in apologetics and it
will be impossible to draw out all of the implications of these
passages. Nevertheless, there are a number of guidelines which
may be suggested at this point. Each of these guidelines is
designed to help the apologist avoid the extremes which often
arise when approaching the non-Christian.

1. Gentle Firmness

It seems inevitable that Christians will come to a non-Christian with too much firmness or too much gentleness. We have seen that Peter says that we should defend the faith with "gentleness" (I Pet. 3:15) and Paul told Timothy "with gentleness correcting those who are in opposition" (II Tim. 2:25). The apologist who seeks to follow these biblical injunctions will sometimes think that gentleness is equivalent to acting uncertain about his allegiance to dependence on God. In these cases the Christian may be tempted to make such statements as, "Well, I don't know for certain that Christianity is true . . ." or "I guess it's possible that I am wrong. . . ." Yet, these believers need to be reminded of the firmness they must have. Gentleness must not compromise but hold firmly to the reliability of the Word of Christ. On the other hand, some Christians, convinced of the need for firmness of conviction, go after the non-Christian with both guns flashing. Seeing themselves as the invincible crusaders, they go after the non-Christian, pursue him without mercy and try to chase him into the kingdom. Such ones need to be reminded of the biblical directive of gentleness in approaching the non-Christian. We do the non-Christian a disservice if we do not offer the demands of the gospel to him with firmness. As we would call to a friend who is about to fall off a cliff, we must be firm with non-Christians. Yet, we must be gentle as well, lest in our enthusiasm we end up pushing him off the cliff rather than saving him from death. The gentle firmness of biblical apologetics may be compared to the careful guidance of a loving friend leading a blind friend to the one place of safety in this world; the safety of Christ.

2. Respectful Challenging

Peter also says that we are to defend the faith with "reverence" (I Pet. 3:15) or respect toward unbelievers. Yet, this notion is also misunderstood by many apologists. Too often, Christians have the idea that respecting the non-Christian for what he is means that they cannot challenge him: "He's so much smarter than I am. I can't even begin to argue with him." It is true that according to human standards a believer might fall beneath the intelligence and prestige of a non-Christian.

> For consider your calling, brethren, that there were not many
> wise according to the flesh, not many mighty, not many noble
> (I Cor. 1:26).

Yet, this does not mean that we should not challenge even the greatest among men. We are to "*respond* to each person" (Col. 4:5, 6), "*correcting* those who are in opposition" (II Tim. 2:25). We must be ready and willing to challenge unbelievers. In fact, one of the most important jobs of the apologist is to challenge the non-Christian in such a way as to show him that he has no cause for pride or confidence in his abilities. We must let him know he is mere man.

Some Christians, however, challenge but fail to have reverence and respect. They say to themselves, "No matter how great he may think he is, this non-Christian is a nobody. He is a fool. I'm the only one with truth." This attitude often shows itself in the student who thinks his non-Christian professors are hopelessly stupid and challenges them with an air of arrogance and superiority. These believers need to be reminded of the scriptural instruction concerning reverence and respect. We are "to malign no one . . . showing every consideration for all men" (Titus 3:2). While we must challenge the non-Christian to forsake his ways of independence and to trust in Christ for salvation, we must do so respectfully. Respectful challenging is an important aspect of a careful approach.

3. Directed Answers

Another problem that often arises when approaching the non-Christian is the tendency to ignore his questions and push the conversation toward a goal of your own or to follow whatever line of thought which he may wish to pursue. On the one hand, there is the perspective that we should "make a defense to every one" (I Pet. 3:15) and that this means no matter what the direction of the conversation it should be followed by the Christian. The desire to be genuine in our concern for the non-Christian's questions is well intended. Yet, there is no biblical support for assuming that we must answer *every* question without exception. Answering every person, as Peter says, is different from answering every question. In fact, Paul told Timothy to "refuse foolish and ignorant speculations, knowing that they produce quarrels"

(II Tim. 2:23). We must be prepared and willing to answer the questions of unbelievers but careful to avoid the sort of questions that lead to nothing but useless argument. Instead, we are to direct our conversations with the unbelieving world so that "God may grant them repentance" (II Tim. 2:25). We must have a definite purpose, leading the lost to Christ. We are not to be interested in showing our own abilities to quarrel and argue. We should choose to answer those questions and follow up those lines of thought which lead the conversation to the issue at hand: belief in Christ and submission to Him as the Lord.

4. Concerned Preparation

The practice of biblical apologetics is a difficult matter to discuss because it involves relating the principles of the Bible to a world of changing circumstances. This difficulty has caused defenders of the faith to go to one extreme or the other. One perspective is that we must be concerned about the individuality of the non-Christian with whom we come in contact to the point that we should avoid all structuring of our approach to apologetics. "There can be no 'system' or 'method' which will always work, so do not prepare a method at all," some may say. As well meaning as these believers may be, they have forgotten the biblical directive for preparation in defending the faith and have failed to realize that only the tremendously creative and specially blessed are able to say anything at all without a previously conceived structure. On the other hand, there are those who see the need for a biblical method and suggest, after some research, a detailed approach to be used in every situation. The words of Paul in Colossians 4:5, 6 speak to this issue. We must walk with "wisdom" toward unbelievers. To act with wisdom, however, we must be "seasoned, as it were, with salt." Then, we will be able to "know how [we] should respond to each person." Wisdom in apologetics involves both the seasoning of biblical preparation for handling situations and the flexibility to meet each situation and person with concern and Christian love. The needs of an older man on his death bed are somewhat different from the needs of a college student. Their questions will be different and we must be ready to answer both individually. With concerned preparation the apologist will be able to handle different people and circumstances in a manner pleasing to God and helpful to his neighbor.

There are numerous other matters which relate to our attitudes and actions when meeting with non-Christians. We have merely touched on a few of the more central issues. Constant review in the light of Scripture is the only way to insure a careful approach, but such an approach will provide the basis for a successful and effective biblical apology.

C. A Correct Procedure

In addition to a consistent life and a careful approach, biblical apologetics must follow a correct procedure as well. The sort of answers we give to the questions of non-Christians are very important to the defense of Christianity. To develop a proper method we must keep in mind the basic principles of Scripture which we have discussed in previous lessons. It will be helpful to mention a few of these again.

1. Biblical apologetics constructs a method based on the teaching of Scripture.

The Bible has a great deal to say about apologetics. It offers a theological background which gives the basis and the goal of defending the faith. The theology of the Bible provides general guidelines which should govern the method of apologetics. Moreover, there are numerous specific references to the sort of procedure to be used by believers when confronted by unbelievers. In addition to all of these helpful insights, the Scriptures contain many examples of how men of God in the past have defended the faith and we must take these examples into account as we develop a correct procedure. Fundamental to biblical apologetics is that it be *biblical.*

2. Biblical apologetics requires that the believer present his case for Christianity with the complete assurance that his faith is true and entirely defensible.

When defending the faith we rest our defense on the truthfulness of Christianity and answer unbelief from that stance. A proper procedure begins with the firm conviction that Jesus is Lord (cf. I Pet. 3:15) and that His Word is true beyond doubt. The

Christian must never admit to the possibility that Christ is not the Lord because he is limited and may discover some new 'fact' which will disprove Christianity. He knows for certain that his faith is true because God, who knows all, has revealed it as such. Christian apologists are often tempted to forsake this principle by arguing that Christianity is merely a "possible hypothesis" or to argue that it is "probably true." Yet, to proceed in this fashion is to admit that it is *possible* that the Christian religion is untrue. Such a method cannot be accepted by the biblical apologist. We must stand firm in our allegiance to dependence on God when we defend our faith.

3. Biblical apologetics must maintain the Creator-creature distinction.

Christians must always remember when defending the faith that human reason is never to be treated as the ultimate or final authority. The goal of apologetics is to have men submit dependently to God and we must not seek to bring them to that point by encouraging the non-Christian to continue setting himself up as judge of the credibility of Christianity. All too often apologetics merely challenges the non-Christian to clean up some of the flaws in his supposed independent reason. Yet, nowhere in Scripture are men told to sit as judges over the claims of Christ; they are consistently exhorted to forsake their foolish ways of rebellion and to acknowledge their total dependence on God.

4. Biblical apologetics gives regard to the effects of sin and regeneration on man's ability to know truly and to make correct moral decisions.

Non-Christians reject God as the source of truth; Christians, on the other hand, acknowledge their dependence on God and His Word seeking to submit their entire being to Him. For this reason, there are no 'neutral facts' upon which the Christian may build a case for the Christian faith. There are no such stepping stones to faith. Christians seek to understand all facts in the light of the Scriptures and non-Christians seek to reject all acknowledgment of God. A proper procedure for defending the faith must recognize this character of all 'facts' and act accordingly.

5. Biblical apologetics seeks to communicate effectively and convince the non-Christian on the basis that he is God's image and is aware of his creatureliness.

The history of apologetics is plagued by the idea that rationality or logic is what makes it possible for the non-Christian to be convinced of Christianity. In fact, in one way or another this has been the difficulty with most apologetic procedures. When following a biblical method we must remember that effective communication comes by the fact that fallen man is still the image of God and therefore knows God even though he refuses to acknowledge Him. Whenever we approach the non-Christian we may have confidence not because he is reasonable or logical. We may speak to him on the basis of what he is and what he already knows.

These five principles form a good background for the further development of a proper procedure in future lessons. If they are kept in mind, a biblical method is not difficult to construct.

In this lesson we have introduced the practice of defending the Christian faith. Though these perspectives were merely preliminary, our life, approach, and procedure are essential aspects of biblical apologetics.

Review Questions:

1. What effects can the various aspects of our Christian *lives* have on our defense?

2. Name three principles to remember when *approaching* the non-Christian. Can you support these from Scripture?

3. What are five biblical principles which should guide our *procedure* when defending the faith? Can you support these from Scripture?

Lesson 9. Popular Tactics

Conduct yourselves with wisdom toward outsiders, making the most of the opportunity. Let your speech be with grace, seasoned, as it were, with salt, so that you may know how you should respond to each person (Col. 4:5–6).

There have been many volumes written throughout the history of the church on the subject of apologetics and as a result various methods for defending the faith have been developed. Paul warned the Colossians to use "wisdom toward outsiders" (Col. 4:5) and if we wish to follow his directive we must examine all approaches to defending the faith by the standard of Scripture. In this lesson, we will look at the approach which has been generally characteristic of most protestant apologetics and which is especially popular among evangelicals and campus organizations. This examination will not be comprehensive but the key issues will be discussed. Though we will be primarily negative in our evaluation of these popular tactics, there is a great deal of good and useful work done by those who have worked so hard in these areas. Their motives are pure and much of their work is worthwhile. Nevertheless, it is important to see the great failures of their method. A small but well-written book which represents the main thrust of much of popular apologetic tactics is *Know Why You Believe* by Paul E. Little. We shall use this book as a guide for our investigation.

A. The Role of Human Reason

A central tenet of popular aplogetics is an unbiblical view of human reason. If there is one issue which could be seen as the most important for Little's defense of Christianity, it is the value placed on the rational capacity of men. As a result, Little entitles the first chapter of his book "Is Christianity Rational?" and suggests that there are two erroneous views on the subject among Christians today. The first he calls "anti-intellectual" for the gospel is seen as "at least nonrational if not irrational."[1] On the other hand, there is the view that becoming a Christian is an "exclusively rational process";[2] there is no more to Christian conversion but mental assent to certain religious notions. These two are "equally erroneous viewpoints."[3]

In response to these extremes Little offers a third point of view. There is the rational element in conversion which consists of the "comprehension of a rational body of truth,"[4] but a moral choice for which one must depend on the Holy Spirit is an additional element of true conversion. As far as Little is concerned, man's problem does not lie in his rational abilities; his problem is choosing for Christianity.

> They don't want to believe it. . . . It is primarily a matter of the will.[5]

Consequently, Little says that

> Faith in Christianity is based on evidence. It is a reasonable faith. Faith in the Christian sense goes beyond reason not against it.[6]

In conclusion, he argues that indeed *"Christianity is rational."*[7]

Little's view of reason has several major difficulties. First, human reason is not seen as entirely dependent on God. Little encourages the Christian apologist to present Christianity as a view to be examined and judged by independent human reason. Faith is not to rest on God's self-testimony but on evidence perceived by independent reason. Second, reason is not seen as affected by the fall of man into sin. Man's problem does not, for Little, include blindness to the truth but his unwillingness to choose the truth which he is fully capable of knowing. As a result, Little treats rationality and logical analysis as something neutral

---

[1] Paul Little, *Know Why You Believe*, (Downers Grove, Ill.: Inter-Varsity Press, 1968), p. 2.
[2] Ibid., p. 3.
[3] Ibid., p. 1.
[4] Ibid., p. 3.
[5] Ibid., p. 4.
[6] Ibid., p. 5.
[7] Ibid., p. 6.

for both Christians and non-Christians. Rational evidences and arguments are the neutral tools by which the unbeliever may be convinced of the credibility of Christianity. As far as Little is concerned, apologists need only to help the unbeliever think more clearly and rationally in his independence and he will be convinced of the truth of Christianity.

Needless to say, this view of human reason contradicts the biblical point of view as it has been explained in previous lessons. The fall of man involved the entirety of man; all aspects of his personality were corrupted by sin. As a result, reason is not the judge of truth; only God can act as such a judge. Moreover, sin has so affected mankind that even rational abilities are not neutral. Christians seek to use their reason in dependence on God. Non-Christians seek to be independent in their thinking; there is no neutral ground on which to deal with unbelief. Human reason can be as much a hindrance as a help to faith in Christ. As St. Augustine once said, "Believe that you may understand." To rest our faith on independent reason is to rebel against God. Reason must rest on our faith commitment to Christ and our faith must rest on God alone.

B. The Manner of Defense

Typical of the sort of defensive tactics which is represented by Little is the tendency to convince the non-Christian of the Christian faith by dealing with three aspects of the faith separately and allowing one issue to lead into the others. These three issues are the existence of God, the deity of Christ, and the authority of Scripture.

1. The Existence of God

Of first priority to Little's approach is the proof of the existence of God. He offers several evidences for the existence of God. First is the fact that "the vast majority of humanity, at all times and in all places, has believed in some kind of god or gods."[8] Second, the law of cause and effect points to a first cause or "uncaused

[8]Ibid., p. 8.

cause."[9] Third, is the argument that the great design of the world points to a divine designer.[10] Though these evidences are mere "indications of God"[11] and not proofs in a strict sense, Little rests his case for belief in the existence of God on these arguments.

The problems with this approach are many. First, Little does not account for the dependence of man's reason on God. In the face of the reality of God's existence the unbeliever is encouraged to act as if he were God and able to judge the question of God's existence independently. The non-Christian, according to Little, does not need to radically change his approach to God's existence; he merely needs to clean up some of the difficulties in his thinking. Second, no recognition is given to the effects of sin on the reasoning processes of the unbeliever. All the arguments in the universe will not bring the unbeliever to the truth; he must be converted. In fact, though the evidences for God's existence presented by Little are convincing to the believer, unbelieving philosophers have discredited and refuted them long ago. From a non-Christian perspective the "evidences" for God's existence are not convincing. Third, Little operates on the assumption that it is possible for reflective unbelievers to see God in creation. The Scriptures, however, teach that all men, even the unreflecting, know the God of Scripture through creation. To try to convince the unbeliever of the existence of a god of some undefined character, as Little does, is to lead him away from what true knowledge of the God of Scripture he already has. For these reasons, to argue for the existence of God as Little has suggested is clearly contrary to the guiding principles of Scripture.

2. The Deity of Christ

Once the existence of a God has been established, Little's next goal is to prove the distinctively Christian notion that Jesus is God revealed in the flesh. He does so by a discussion of Christ's own claims to divinity and the miracle of the resurrection. There are, according to Little, four possible ways of reacting to Jesus' self-testimony. He is either a liar, a lunatic, a legend, or truly God in the flesh. In response to the notion that Jesus was a liar Little says,

[9]Ibid., p. 9.
[10]Ibid., p. 10.
[11]Ibid., p. 12.

> Even those who deny his deity affirm that they think Jesus was
> a great moral teacher. They fail to realize those two statements
> are a contradiction.[12]

To the idea that Jesus was a lunatic he argues,

> But as we look at the life of Christ, we see no evidence of
> abnormality and unbalance we find in the deranged person.[13]

In response to the idea that Jesus' claim of divinity is mere
legend, Little contends

> The legend theory does not hold water in the light of the early
> date of the Gospel manuscripts.[14]

So, in conclusion Little claims that "the only other alternative is
that Jesus spoke the truth."[15]

Once again Little's arguments fail to challenge the unbeliever.
Instead of insisting on the necessity of repentance and faith as
the ground for true knowledge, Little acts as if the unbeliever
needs merely to be logical about Jesus' claims in order to arrive at
the truth. While his insights are valuable for the Christian and
are in many respects helpful for defending the faith, they can
certainly be refuted from a non-Christian stance. Little has not
ruled out the possibility from a sinful perspective for thinking of
Christ as liar, lunatic, or legend. Not all unbelievers believe Jesus
was a great moral teacher. Not all would agree that the unusual
life which Jesus led is different in quality from lunacy. Not all
non-Christians would accept the recent dating of the gospel
records as convincing evidence of the factual nature of their
content, especially in supernatural and miraculous matters.
Moreover, unbelievers will certainly never be logically forced into
believing Christ is truly the divine Son of God. Little's motives are
worthwhile, but his approach falls short of the biblical principles
relevant to defending the faith.

Beyond Christ's own words about His deity, Little also appeals
to the resurrection of Christ as proof of His divinity. It is true
that

> Jesus' supreme credential to authenticate his claim to deity was
> his resurrection from the dead.[16]

---

[12]Ibid., p. 17.
[13]Ibid., p. 18.
[14]Ibid.

[15]Ibid.
[16]Ibid., p. 21.

If Christ had not been raised then our faith as Christians would be of no avail. Yet, Little misunderstands this centrality of the resurrection to mean that if Christ's resurrection can be proven historically, the deity of Christ is proven. He seeks by various means to dispel false notions about the resurrection. Appealing to the biblical record as his guideline, he argues that the empty tomb is the irrefutable proof of Christian truth. The body of Christ could not have been stolen. The women could not have gone to the wrong tomb. Jesus had to have been actually dead, and His resurrection could not have been an hallucination. As far as Little is concerned,

> The only theory that adequately explains the empty tomb is the resurrection of Jesus Christ from the dead. [17]

Again, Little's arguments are sound from a Christian perspective but they hold little or no weight for non-Christians. One obvious way in which this can be seen is that Little "refutes" the various explanations of the resurrection on the basis of biblical data, the very source of information being called into question. For instance, in response to the idea that Jesus was buried alive, Little argues that if it had been so the wrappings on Christ's body and the stone before the tomb would have been obstacles too great for a weak man to overcome. It is obvious, however, that if the unbeliever is going to question the accuracy of the biblical account regarding Christ's death, it is hardly adequate to answer his view with other portions of the biblical account. That argument alone will not answer the objection of the non-Christian adequately. Moreover, even if Little could prove the historicity of the resurrection, he has not proven the deity of Christ. The Bible and other religious traditions claim that many people have been resurrected from the dead. Moreover, we can attach whatever meaning we wish to an empty tomb. Without the scriptural information about the resurrection, it could mean any number of things. In fact, the unbelieving heart will attribute any other significance to the empty tomb than the correct and biblical significance, even if it means putting the resurrection among those unexplainable events in *Ripley's Believe It or Not!* Apart from dependence on the revelation of God, the resurrection proves nothing. This is why Peter did not take his Jerusalem audience on the day of Pentecost to the empty tomb and say, "See, the tomb is empty.

[17]Ibid., p. 27.

Now disprove that Jesus is the Christ!" He knew that false interpretations of the empty tomb had already begun to circulate. Instead he referred his Jewish brothers to the Old Testament prophecy of the event saying

> The Lord said to my Lord, "sit at My right hand, until I make Thine enemies a footstool for Thy feet" (Acts 2:34–35).

We must remember this same factor when relating the message of Christ's resurrection today. If stripped of its biblical meaning, the resurrection proves nothing. If declared in the context of biblical truth, it is the foundation of saving faith. Finally, what has been said before about Little's method applies here as well. Unbelievers are not to be led to faith in Christ by being encouraged to think independently. Essentially, Little's approach urges the non-Christian to examine the truth of God about the resurrection by the criterion of history and logic. Whatever biblical information is introduced is done so without acknowledgment of the need for total dependence on it. Consequently, this tactic for defending Christ's resurrection and His divinity is inadequate.

3. The Authority of Scripture

The final stage of Little's apology is the defense of biblical authority. Little spends a great deal of time on this subject. He begins by citing the Bible's own testimony to its divine authorship. He cautions the reader, however, saying,

> While the statements and claims of the Scriptures are not proof of themselves, they are a significant body of data which cannot be ignored.[18]

After illustrating his point from the text of Scripture, Little concludes,

> There are, then, a number of pieces of evidence on which one can reasonably base his belief that the Bible is the Word of God.[19]

Moreover, he discusses the preservation and reliability of the texts of both the Old and New Testaments. Archeology and science are reported to support biblical authority and to give no evidence against it. In this regard, however, Little correctly asserts

[18]Ibid., p. 31.
[19]Ibid., p. 38.

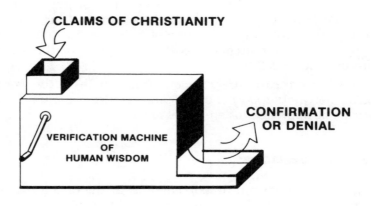

CLAIMS OF CHRISTIANITY

VERIFICATION MACHINE
OF
HUMAN WISDOM

CONFIRMATION
OR DENIAL

Figure 20

In everything we read and in everything we hear we must ask,
"What is this person's presuppostion?" so that we may interpret
his conclusion in this light.[20]

Even so, there is little or no effort to put these kinds of observations
into practice when defending the Scriptures. Nowhere does Little
suggest that Christian and non-Christian presuppositions about
the Bible's relation to science are fundamentally different. There
are only slight differences. The authority of the Scriptures remains
contingent, at least theoretically, on every discovery of science;
Little's apology cannot keep the credibility of the Bible which he
proves by the evidence of science, from being destroyed by that
same science when the so-called evidence is to the contrary.
Biblical authority must never depend on human verification for
it is the unquestionable Word of God.

The problem with much of the popular tactics used by many
defenders of the faith today may be summed up as a problem of
authority. The apologist must see clearly that the non-Christian
is in need of forsaking his commitment to independence and
should turn in faith to the authority of Christ. If, however, trust
in Christ is founded on logical consistency, historical evidence,
scientific arguments, etc., then Christ is yet to be received as the
ultimate authority. The various foundations are more authoritative

[20]Ibid., p. 79.

than Christ Himself. To use yet another analogy, if belief in Christian truth comes only after the claims of Christ are run through the verification machine of independent human judgment, then human judgment is still thought to be the ultimate authority (see Fig. 20).

So, while we can surely benefit from much of the work of apologists who support these popular tactics, we must forsake their basic approach for a biblical apology.

Review Questions:

1. Why is it important to look carefully at the various ways for defending the faith that are suggested today?
2. Describe the role of human reason in Little's approach to apologetics.
3. What are the three steps in Little's method?
4. What are several criticisms of Little's view which should be remembered?

Lesson 10. The Basic Structure of a Biblical Defense

Answer not a fool according to his folly, lest you be like him yourself. Answer a fool according to his folly, lest he be wise in his own eyes (Prov. 26:4, 5).

Observing the mistakes made by others in apologetics, as we have done in the last lesson, is certainly worthwhile, but a more important task is the positive development of a biblical defense of Christianity. In this lesson we will seek to propose the basic structure of an apology which takes into consideration the directives found in Scripture. Before we begin, however, it must be remembered that the Bible does not give us step-by-step instructions for defending the faith. It is therefore necessary to acknowledge that the structure suggested in this lesson is only one among many which adequately accounts for the biblical principles involved. The suggestions of this lesson may be helpful to some and not to others. Moreover, at times only some of these ideas will be suitable for particular situations. Whatever optional approaches are adopted, however, we must be certain that the method is in line with the biblical principles we have discussed in previous lessons.

A. Evangelism and Apologetics

A significant matter for the structure of a biblical defense is the relation of apologetics and evangelism. Many unbiblical practices rise from misunderstanding this relationship and valuable insights can be found by a correct perspective. Evangelism and apologetics are similar in several respects. Both are responsibilities which rest to some extent on all believers. All believers are to spread the gospel of Christ and defend it by their deeds and words. Evangelism and apologetics both assume that there is a degree of willingness on the part of the unbeliever to hear and discuss the claims of Christ on his life. Neither the evangelist nor the apologist should throw his precious pearls of truth before those who wish to do nothing but make a mockery of Christ (cf. Matt. 7:6). In both areas the Christian is dealing with the issues of life and death. Many think of apologetics as a mere intellectual game where nothing is at stake but winning or losing an argument. Yet, as we have said before, in apologetics we offer to the unbeliever the choice of salvation or judgment, even as we do in evangelism. In this same way, biblical apologetics can no more guarantee the conversion of the lost than can biblical evangelism. In spite of all our efforts and our most profound arguments the unbeliever will not be won unless he is touched by God's grace and is made willing to believe from his heart. Learning about apologetics will not make anyone an automatic soul winner; only God's grace can make the gospel effective. These close connections between evangelism and apologetics can be seen by the way in which they are related to each other in Scripture. In Acts 26:2 we are told that Paul made a defense before King Agrippa but he offers as a vital part, if not the climax of his defense, the gospel of Christ, saying

> that the Christ was to suffer, and that by reason of His resurrection from the dead He should be the first to proclaim light both to the Jewish people and to the Gentiles (Acts 26:23).

Moreover, when Paul wrote to Timothy of his first defense of Christianity, he mentioned that he had hoped that in his defense "the proclamation might be fully accomplished, and that all the Gentiles might hear" (II Tim. 4:17). In other words, Paul's apology was complete only as it fulfilled the need of the proclamation of the gospel to the Gentiles. In whatever circumstances we may be, the defense of the faith must be intertwined with the declaration of the good news that salvation from sin and death has come through the death and resurrection of Jesus, the Son of God.

If the similarities which apologetics and evangelism share are kept in mind, a common misconception may be avoided. Apologetics is not an attempt to confront only the mind of the non-Christian while leaving the will and emotions to evangelism.

When we defend the faith properly we do not merely argue for Christianity in preparation for a later step of challenging the unbeliever to turn to Christ for salvation. Instead, apologetics confronts the entire personality of the unbeliever with the demands of God in Christ. Defending the gospel does not merely precede the offer of the gospel; it entails the declaration of the gospel.

While it is important to give heed to the affinity of apologetics and evangelism, it is necessary to make some distinction as well. Unless we do so, one of two tendencies may result. On the one hand, the believer may tend to forsake all attempts at defending the faith and merely substitute preaching the faith. If apologetics and evangelism are entirely the same, the Christian may refuse to answer the questions of unbelief and simply say, "You must believe what I am saying because you must believe!" This procedure, needless to say, is far from that of Christ and His apostles who took seriously the objections of their opponents. On the other hand, failure to distinguish apologetics and evangelism may cause the Christian to think that he must go through a long and elaborate defense before Christ can be trusted by the unbeliever. If a non-Christian were to approach such a Christian and say that he wanted to believe, the Christian might respond, "Wait a minute! You can't really believe until I have answered the objections others usually raise against faith in Christ." We must remember that in response to a similar situation Paul simply replied, "Believe in the Lord Jesus, and you shall be saved" (Acts 16:31). The total identification of apologetics with evangelism will often lead to unbiblical methods and practices. Care must be taken to distinguish one from the other.

It is helpful to view the difference between apologetics and evangelism as one of thrust or intention. Evangelism is directed more toward the *proclamation* of the judgment to come and the good news of salvation in the death and resurrection of Christ. The unbeliever is told in no uncertain terms

> He who believes in the Son has eternal life; but he who does not obey the Son shall not see life, but the wrath of God abides on him (John 3:36).

Apologetics, however, is more concerned with the *justification* of these claims. We make a defense "to every one who asks [us] to give an account for the hope that is in [us]" (I Pet. 3:15). In this

CONVERSION OF LOST

Figure 21

sense, it may be said that evangelism deals more with *what* we should believe and apologetics more with *why* we should believe. To be sure, there is certainly a great deal of common concern for both fields, but we may think of apologetics as *extended evangelism* for it seeks to defend and convince the unbeliever of the message of judgment and hope as it is presented in the gospel (see Fig. 21).

On this basis, we are able to point out more clearly how to begin and end the defense of Christianity. As we have already noted, in I Peter 3:15 we are told that our preparation for defense is to be put into effect when we are called on to answer *why* we have Christian hope. In ordinary conversations with unbelievers apologetic opportunities may arise as a result of the discussion of a particular issue or matter of controversy. When the Christian gives his view of the matter, he may have the opportunity to show that his opinion stems from his Christian faith and at that point

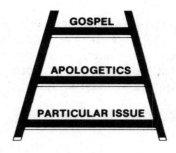

Figure 22

be able to defend his allegiance to dependence on Christ. At the end of his defense will be the challenge for the unbeliever to submit to the good news of Christ (see Fig. 22).

For instance, a believer may express his opinion on war, capital punishment, or any other issue. Whatever particular responses may be given, if the conversation continues long enough, the believer will become involved in defending his commitment to Christ from which his opinion stems. Once the defense has begun, it must be intertwined with the gospel and must lead to effectively challenging the independence of sinful man and calling him to repentance. Apologetics is brought into the Christian/non-Christian dialogue when the need for defense arises and serves to bring to bear in an effective and convincing way the good news of Christ.

B. The Twofold Justification

Proverbs 26:4, 5 offer some helpful instructions for justifying the claims of the gospel. There is a wealth of practical instruction contained in these verses; in both we are told how to answer the fool. The book of Proverbs has much to say about the fool. Essentially, he is one who questions the trustworthiness of God's wisdom revealed to man. He has rejected the fear of God and thus all wisdom. For our purposes, the fool may be thought of as a non-Christian who is asking for a defense of the Christian faith. We are told, on the one hand, not to "answer a fool according to his folly" (v. 4). In other words, we are to answer the non-Christian without forsaking our dependence on God's revelation; we must answer from the perspective of Christian philosophy.

On the other hand, the proverb teaches that we should "answer a fool according to his folly" (v. 5).[1] There is a sense in which we must defend the Christian faith by using the perspective of non-Christian philosophy. We shall look at both of these means of justifying the claims of the Christian faith.

1. Argument by Truth

Argument by truth is basically answering the non-Christian's objections and questions about the credibility of Christian claims from the Christian or biblical perspective. Notice why the writer of Proverbs says we should argue by truth.

> Answer not a fool according to his folly, lest you be like him yourself (Prov. 26:4).

The foolish unbeliever has no hope for release from the effects of sin in his life. He cannot find God by his philosophy and he cannot even know himself or the world correctly. If the Christian fails to recognize the importance of argument by truth, he too will be bound up in the same futility. Too often, Christians try to justify Christianity by denying it in their apologetic method and thus become like the foolish unbeliever. Such confusion will be avoided if we give proper place to argument by truth. In Athens, Paul began his defense by arguing from the Christian perspective for the true character of God. He said,

> What therefore you worship in ignorance, this I proclaim to you. The God who made the world and all things in it, since He is the Lord of heaven and earth, does not dwell in temples made with hands . . . (Acts 17:23–24).

Also, in Acts 22 Paul began his defense by presenting his conversion story from the Christian perspective. Whether or not we actually begin with argument by truth in every situation is unimportant, but we should be certain never to forsake it for this sort of argument is essential to biblical apologetics.

By arguing from the Christian perspective, the Christian is able to show that commitment to dependence on God is not self-frustrating and enables a person to live free from the futility of sin's dominion. As Paul said,

---

[1]The NASB translation of this passage fails to render the meaning of the original. I have followed the RSV.

I am not out of my mind . . . but I utter words of sober truth (Acts 26:25).

Argument by truth can and will take on different forms as we approach different situations, but no matter what form is given, the response must be according to the revelation of God in Scripture. For this reason it is imperative that the defender of the faith be well studied and familiar with the Bible. One can hardly argue by truth if he is ignorant of truth. Every aspect of biblical revelation is able to be used in apologetics, and the effectiveness of the apologist will depend to a great extent on his ability to handle accurately "the Word of truth" (II Tim. 2:15). In the Word of God lies the truth of the Spirit which will convince the unbeliever of his need of the Savior and the sufficiency of Christ's death and resurrection for salvation. As obedient servants we must "answer not a fool according to his folly" but according to the truth of God's Word.

There are basically three steps in the argument by truth. *First,* the Christian should admit that his answer stems from his trust in Christ as Lord and Savior. This confession can take the form of a simple statement or the more elaborate narrative of one's conversion experience. Whatever the case, one of the best ways to avoid much of the confusion which could arise by omitting this step is to begin the argument by truth with a clear statement of fundamental commitment to Christ.

The *second* step of the argument by truth may take one of two forms. If, on the one hand, the apologist does not know the biblical data for a Christian response, he should not be discouraged. Christianity provides an explanation even for our ignorance. We may be ignorant because of our finiteness as human beings. Yet, we can be sure that if an answer is to be found it must be done by dependence on the revelation of God. For instance, most Christians do not know about all the so-called scientific evidence for and against evolution. Yet, this in no way calls into question the certainty of the biblical record of creation. While the Christian may not know all, he knows the source of all and can rest confident in the Creator of heaven and earth and oppose the falsehoods of disbelief. The unknown is in no way a threat to that which is known from God's Word, for God knows all without exception; and His revelation is totally reliable. However the argument by truth may proceed in actual situations, it is nevertheless argument by *truth*—truth which never fails—and it should be presented as such even in the face of great ignorance.

On the other hand, if the believer knows the Christian answer to the unbeliever's objection, he should go about justifying the Christian position. The establishment of the Christian point of view certainly involves referring to the Bible and the answers contained there, but much more is to be included in the argument by truth. When seen in the light of Scripture, the external world and the Christian's personal experience and reflection support the Christian stance. The world and man are what the Bible says they are, and the Christian should use these aspects of creation to illustrate and support the biblical position. This is not to say that the evidences found outside the Bible are neutral tools to be used without recognition of the true nature of religious commitments. These sorts of evidences are just as religiously conditioned as the biblical evidences. As believers in Christ we are convinced that the Bible speaks truly with regard to the world and the believer's private experiences, and that this correspondance between Scripture and life can be seen from the Christian stance as an example of the way in which Christianity escapes the futility of sinful thought. It is in this way that we may understand the apostle Paul's defense of the resurrection of Christ in I Corinthians 15:3-8. Essentially, there are three levels of argument used by Paul in this passage. First (vv. 3-4), he argued that Christ's death, burial, and resurrection are according to the Old Testament Scripture and apostolic tradition. "He was raised on the third day according to the Scriptures" (I Cor. 15:4), Paul urged. Second (vv. 5-7), he offered an external historical argument supported by the claims of many eyewitnesses. He declared boldly that Christ "appeared to more than five hundred brethren at one time" (I Cor. 15:6). Third (v. 8), Paul supported the truthfulness of Christ's resurrection from his own private experience on the road to Damascus. "He appeared to me also" (I Cor. 15:8). We must be sure to see that Paul is arguing from a distinctively Christian point of view and not from a neutral stance. Moreover, we should take notice of the fact that Paul does not argue for the mere probability of the resurrection. The evidence of Scripture makes certain the reality of Christ's resurrection. While this is so, we must also be aware of the fact that the apostle did not hesitate to use extra-biblical evidence in light of Scripture. In line with the example of Paul, there are basically three sources of evidences which may be used in the argument by truth. We may support the Christian claim with evidence from Scripture, from the external world, and from our personal experience. We shall look rather carefully at each of these sources of evidence.

Evidence from Scripture

The Christian looks to Scripture for divine authority in the questions he must answer. Consequently, supporting the Christian view with scriptural evidence is in many ways the most fundamental of all manners of support. To give evidence for a view from Scripture does not merely mean being able to quote a verse which "proves" the point in question. Very often such a method actually proves nothing. Finding biblical support for a position is also accomplished by relating the biblical principles, or what may be called the *biblical logic*, to the questions of concern. Whatever the case, when the Christian has correctly understood the issues and the biblical support for a position, his view has been supported. In Scripture is found the voice of God speaking to the questions and debates which are so important to the defense of Christianity.

Evidence from the External World

When seen in the light of Scripture, the external world provides many evidences for the Christian point of view. Of course, great caution should be exercised when using these sorts of evidences, for many times even the believer will fail to understand the world around him correctly. Evidences in the external world are sometimes shown to prove something other than they were thought to prove. For instance, in years past it could have been argued by unsuspecting Christians that the revolution of the sun around the earth "proved" the centrality of the earth and her inhabitants in God's plan for the universe. Today, however, science has shown that the earth actually revolves around the sun. What was once incorrectly used as an evidence for Christianity is no longer acceptable, even to the Christian. So, attention must be given to the exercise of care and restraint in the use of evidences from the external world.

While we must be careful, external evidences should be used

whenever possible in the defense of Christianity. The Christian religion does affect the way in which the believer views the external world and this fact should be made clear. Christians do not, as some modern theologians have suggested, believe in Christianity in spite of the facts. They believe because of the facts and only in spite of the *misinterpretations* of the facts by sinful men. This perspective allows and calls for the proper use of scientific, historical, and logical arguments for the Christian point of view. There is the tendency for Christian apologists to make the case for Christianity stand or fall on these evidences. Such a view forsakes the only way of true understanding of the evidences, commitment to Christ and His Word. On the other hand, some believers who wish to hold firmly to their commitment think that there is no role for evidences of the sort described here. Yet, this perspective fails to see the far reaching significance of the sufficient authority of Scripture as it makes clear the true character of the world. The biblical position is that external evidences are important. Paul used them often. For instance, he appealed to the knowledge of God in the Lycaonians by pointing to the order of the external world and saying,

> He [God] did not leave Himself without witness, in that He did good and gave you rains from heaven and fruitful seasons, satisfying your hearts with food and gladness (Acts 14:17).

He also remarked to Festus,

> . . . this has not been done in a corner (Acts 26:26).

The gospel of John lays great stress on the historical evidences or signs of Jesus' divinity. John says plainly,

> Many other signs therefore Jesus also performed . . . ; but these have been written that you may believe . . . (John 20:30–31).

If used correctly, external evidences are a vital part of the argument by truth.

Evidence From Personal Experience

There is yet one other source of evidence which the believer may use in an argument by truth: the evidence of his own personal experience of the Christian faith. Evidences from the external world are usually subject to public inspection of one sort or another, but evidences from personal experience are usually of a private sort. Such aspects of private life as one's conversion experience and the growing and personal relationship of the believer with His God are two of the more prominent arguments to be used. Very often Paul defended the faith by telling of his Damascus road experience (Acts 26:12–20). He presented his private encounter with Christ as a matter of fact which was to be accepted as true on the basis of his claim. Of course, there is to be the external evidence of true conversion in the changing life of the believer, but the conversion and continuing intimacy of the Holy Spirit are sources of undeniable evidence for the Christian view of things.

After the presentation of evidences we are brought to the *third* step in the argument by truth. It should be obvious that in most cases the unbeliever is not going to be satisfied with the justification given in the second step of the argument by truth. In such cases, the argument by truth must go one step further. Once the biblical defense has been given it is necessary to expose the fact that the non-Christian rejects the Christian evidence because of his commitment to independence. Every thought contrary to Christianity which the unbeliever has results from his desire to set himself up as the independent judge of truth. We live in a day when many non-Christians think they are neutral and objective. So, their basic commitment must be exposed. This can be done by a series of questions. If the Christian wishes to show the non-Christian that he has committed himself to independence he may simply assert that it is the case and then ask, "Why do you believe that?" or "How do you know that?" again and again until the point becomes obvious. The unbeliever thinks and believes as he does because he has determined it to be correct independently. For instance, the unbeliever may argue that the Christian God does not exist. When asked "Why?" he may say, "You have shown me no convincing evidence." When asked *why* he thinks the evidence is unconvincing, he will have to admit that the evidence does not meet with his independent criterion of truth. When asked *why* he accepts his criterion of truth he can be shown that it is the result of his own independent decision to look at things without submission to the Bible and to God (see Fig. 23).

By exposing the commitment of the unbeliever, the Christian reveals the truth that all men have either chosen for Christ or against Him. The line of division is clearly drawn and the door is opened for demonstrating the hopelessness of the non-Christian way of thinking.

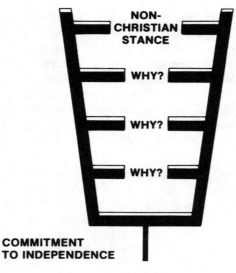

Figure 23

By way of summary, the argument by truth may be seen as answering the non-Christian's objections with Christian responses. There are basically three steps. First, the Christian should admit that all his opinions are regulated by his faith in Christ. Second, he should give the Christian evidence or the explanation of his ignorance on the particular issue at hand. Third, he should show why the non-Christian will not accept the Christian view—because of his sinful self-allegiance. With these three steps in mind, it should not be difficult to construct an argument by truth for the defense of Christianity.

2. Argument by Folly

Proverbs 26:4, 5 also says that we should argue by folly. We are to answer the unbeliever by his own precepts and ideas. Yet, the purpose for such argumentation is not the positive establishment of the Christian view but the demonstration of the foolishness of sinful thought.

> Answer a fool according to his folly, lest he be wise in his own eyes (Prov. 26:5).

The Christian apologist seeks to use the evidences and arguments acceptable to the unbeliever's system in order to remove the non-

Christian's confidence in himself. The non-Christian has no wisdom and his self-confidence is mere deception. The disenchantment of the unbeliever with his way of thinking comes about as the Christian effectively shows him that his rejection of Christ is based on a self-contradicting and self-frustrating perspective which can therefore never lead to true knowledge of himself, the world, or God. Non-Christian philosophy is under the judgment of God and cannot help but be self-defeating. Jeremiah spoke of the inevitable reproach to sinful thought saying,

> Your own wickedness will correct you, and your apostasies will reprove you; Know therefore and see that it is evil and bitter for you to forsake the Lord your God (Jer. 2:19).

Those who forsake God are corrected and reproved by their own efforts. The Psalmist likewise prayed,

> Hold them guilty, O God; By their own devices let them fall! (Ps. 5:10).

Moreover, we read,

> The nations are sunk down in the pit they have made; in the net which they hid, their own foot has been caught. The Lord has made Himself known; He has executed judgment. In the work of his own hands the wicked is snared (Ps. 9:15, 16).

All the scheming, craftiness, and efforts of unbelievers turn against themselves as the judgment of God is revealed to them. This inherent futility is shown to the non-Christian by the believer as he points to the internal inconsistencies within the unbelieving system of thought. In this capacity the apologist becomes a messenger of judgment revealing to his opponent the hopelessness and futility of his rejection of Christ.

As with the argument by truth, the argument by folly has three basic steps. Having already exposed the fact that the unbeliever has committed himself to independence from God, the futility of his position may be shown by asking him to justify that allegiance. If the unbeliever tries to justify it or tries to argue that his independence needs no justification, it is not difficult to show that his response is itself based on his commitment to independence by asking why he thinks his response has validity. In so doing, the unbeliever has given no justification; he has merely illustrated how his allegiance to independence is all pervasive. If the unbeliever argues that his commitment to independence is not able to be justified, then the believer may ask him why he holds it so dear. Whatever the case, it is not difficult to show the non-Christian that he has committed himself blindly to independence and has categorically denied Christianity with no justifiable reason. Moreover, the non-Christian is himself left in the frustration of wishing to hold to a reasonable position against Christianity while being caught in a vicious circle of self-defeat, a circle which can be broken only by believing the gospel.

The non-Christian indeed reasons circularly but the Christian does so as well. The second and third steps in the argument by folly seek to make plain that Christian circularity and non-Christian circularity are radically different. The former provides the fulfillment of man's purpose on earth, and the latter throws the unbeliever into a whirl of inconsistencies and self-contradictions. The futility of disbelief is evident not only in the groundlessness of commitment to independence; it is also discernible in the particular objections which non-Christians may offer against Christianity.

The second step in the argument by folly will take one of two forms depending on the sort of objection which the unbeliever raises. If, on the one hand, the unbeliever makes a claim of *absolute certainty* he should be shown the *total uncertainty* of his statement. If, on the other hand, the unbeliever makes a claim of *total uncertainty*, he should be shown the *absolute certainty* of his position. In other words, the unbeliever should be shown that his own point of view defeats itself by being absolutely certain and totally uncertain at the same time. We shall see how this is the case with regard to the non-Christian view of God, the world, and man.

Objections Regarding God and His Revelation

The unbeliever cannot have any certainty about his view of God and His revelation because he has not known and *cannot* know exhaustively all of creation, much less God Himself. His ignorance forces him to be totally uncertain. The non-Christian, however, cannot be uncertain either, for to be uncertain is to be *certainly uncertain,* and the unbeliever cannot have such certainty. Most non-Christians can be shown the reality of this dilemma by pointing out their ignorance in religious matters. They cannot speak consistently about God or His revelation.

Objections Regarding the World

Very often non-Christians will object to Christianity on the basis of a consideration regarding the external world. Even so, the unbeliever cannot hold a position of certainty because he is unable to account for all the factors and contingencies of the universe. Yet, he cannot be uncertain either for such a position speaks with certainty about the character of the world. The unbeliever cannot but fall into this dilemma. There are always new ideas and new discoveries about the world which leave the unbeliever in a position of being both absolutely certain and totally uncertain. It is impossible for him to escape this problem.

Objections Regarding Man

In a similar way, every non-Christian position of certainty regarding man is totally uncertain and every position of uncertainty is absolutely certain. Consequently, when the unbeliever objects to Christianity on the account of his view of man, he may be shown to be unable to hold his position consistently.

The second step of the argument by folly may be summarized as follows. The Christian may seek to show the inability of the non-Christian to have certainty by pointing out that the non-Christian *has not* examined all of the evidence in the universe. He may do this by referring to some things that the non-Christian would consider acceptable evidence which point in favor of the Christian view. More importantly, however, the Christian should point out that the unbeliever *cannot* examine all the evidence; his finiteness makes a thorough examination impossible. Since some unknown fact may prove his limited understanding to be mistaken, the non-Christian cannot be certain at all that the evidence is truly against the Christian position. If he wishes to hold his position, he does so by blindly choosing against Christ, not because of the evidence.

On the other hand, the position of total uncertainty can be summarized by saying that there is not enough evidence to be sure one way or the other. "You're too dogmatic," the unbeliever may say to the Christian. "We can't be so sure about these things." At first it may seem that this objection is not as bold as the response mentioned above. Yet, it must be seen that when the

A Suggested Structure for a Biblical Apology

A particular issue often gives rise to the presentation of the gospel and an opportunity to defend the Christian faith.

↓

Admit your faith commitment.

ARGUMENT BY TRUTH

DEPENDENT CERTAINTY

If answer is known, give biblical answer and biblical evidence for the particular issue in question.

DEPENDENT UNCERTAINTY

If answer is not known, give justification of your ignorance and show why Christianity is no less certain.

If the unbeliever is not convinced, show him that his disbelief is founded on his commitment to independence.

↓

Show that commitment to independence cannot be justified.

ARGUMENT BY FOLLY

ABSOLUTE CERTAINTY

If the unbeliever is certain, that the evidence is against Christianity, show him that he *has not* and *cannot* know enough to be sure he understands his evidence correctly.

TOTAL UNCERTAINTY

If the unbeliever is uncertain because there is not enough evidence to be sure, show him that he *has not* and *cannot* know enough to be sure that he must be uncertain.

Challenge the unbeliever to recognize his commitment to independence as the source of his futility.

↓

Present the gospel message of repentance and faith.

Figure 24

96

non-Christian says there is not enough evidence, he is not differing in his basic thrust with the unbeliever who says that the evidence is against Christianity. The former is as opposed to the faith as is the latter. One of the best ways of illustrating this to the unbeliever is to respond to his objection by saying, "You haven't seen enough evidence to know for sure that we must be unsure." If the unbeliever answers that he is unsure about his objection as well, then his response is no objection at all. It is merely the expression of personal doubt, not the necessity of doubt. In this light we can see that the unbeliever can neither argue that the evidence is against Christianity nor that there is not enough evidence because he cannot be sure of either statement. The unsaved man is caught in an unending dilemma. He cannot be certain or uncertain consistently. He is caught by his own devices.

The third step of the argument by folly makes obvious why the unbeliever faces futility. It is because of his commitment to independence, his denial of the Creator-creature distinction, that he is caught by his own system. In closing the argument by folly, the Christian should challenge the unbeliever's commitment to independence. The rebel against God must be confronted with his need for repentance and faith in Christ. So, while in many cases a biblical apology begins with the gospel, it most certainly should end with it (see Fig. 24).

The items in this lesson are important though they have been covered only in outline form. Examples will be given in the lessons which follow. Caution must be taken in these matters for there are many considerations which may make it necessary for the structure outlined here to be altered or shortened. Nevertheless, all issues discussed in this lesson should be mastered by the believer to the best of his ability. A knowledge of the basic structure suggested here will often prove to be indispensable to the Christian apologist.

Review Questions:

1. How are apologetics and evangelism similar? Dissimilar?
2. Why may we call apologetics "extended evangelism?"
3. When should we begin our defense of the faith?

4. What is the twofold presentation described in Proverbs 26:4, 5?

5. What are the three basic steps in the argument by truth?

6. What are the three basic steps in the argument by folly?

7. How should a biblical defense begin and end?

Lesson 11. Defending the Faith (1)

> We are destroying speculations and every lofty thing raised up against the knowledge of God, and we are taking captive every thought to the obedience of Christ (II Cor. 10:5)

Having seen the basic structure of biblical apologetics, it is necessary to get down to specifics. In this and the next two lessons we will deal with some of the issues that may come up in conversations with unbelievers. It must be remembered that we will be looking at only a sampling of possible objections and answers. The purpose of these lessons is to give some helpful and basic suggestions for an effective biblical apologetic. The sort of responses that may be offered are limited only by the ability of the apologist, who will learn to develop his own arguments as he becomes experienced in defending the faith.

A. Objections About God

It is obvious that one of the key issues in apologetics is God. It is often the case that the need for apologetics arises because of questions about God Himself.

1. The Existence of God

There is hardly a more basic issue of controversy between Christians and non-Christians than the existence of God. Though the objection may be put in many different forms, very often the unbeliever asks, "Why should I believe that the Christian God exists?"

a. Argument by Truth

There are three steps to the argument by truth. Each one of these is important to the defense of the existence of God.

Step 1: The Christian should admit that his fundamental reason for belief in the existence of the Christian God is his faith in Christ.

Step 2: The apologist should then proceed to offer the Christian evidence for belief in the existence of God.

Evidence from Scripture

1) The Bible assumes the existence of God and operates on the reality of His existence without long drawn out proofs (Gen. 1:1). Even if there were no external evidences for God's existence He would still exist.

2) Belief in the existence of God is the beginning of all wisdom and understanding (Prov. 1:8). It is He who is the ground of true understanding, not the construction of reason.

3) The Scriptures teach that only a fool would deny the existence of God (Ps. 14:1). You have to be blind not to see the necessity of God's existence. Without God, nothing else would be, not even the questioning of His existence.

4) The fact that the prophecies of the Old and New Testaments were and are being fulfilled shows that the Christian God exists and is working all things by His own will.

Evidence from the External World

5) God is clearly revealed in the nature of the world (Ps. 19:1; Rom. 1:18). The order of the world points to God's ordering wisdom. The good things in the world show God's mercy. The beauty of the world shows the glory of God. The world around us gives plenty of proof for belief in the existence of God.

6) The grand abilities of men give a demonstration of God's existence and Creatorhood.

Evidence from Personal Experience

7) The Christian also knows that God exists because He has given His grace to him and made His presence known unmistakably by the message of the gospel. There are many Christians who have experienced the wondrous presence of God; they know and claim with certainty that God exists.

Step 3: The believer must recognize that in many situations these arguments will not be convincing. So, he must inform the unbeliever that these arguments are not convincing because of his basic allegiance to independence. He may then proceed to expose that commitment by the process mentioned in the last lesson.

b. Argument by Folly

In this case the argument by folly will seek to show the unbeliever that he has no solid basis upon which he may reject belief in the existence of the Christian God.

Step 1: The Christian should show that the unbeliever's commitment to independence upon which all of his objections rest is not able to be justified. The unbeliever is caught in his own trap.

Step 2: The specific position taken by the non-Christian may also be shown to be self-refuting.

Positions Claiming Absolute Certainty

"There is no god."

1) Show the unbeliever that he has not looked and cannot look everywhere for God.

2) The unbeliever must be shown that he cannot say with certainty, "There is no god" because the convincing evidence for God may be in the place he has not looked for it.

"There is a god but not the Christian God."

1) The believer may ask what sort of God the non-Christian believes in and may then show him that he has not dealt with all the possible evidences for God's character.

2) The unbeliever should be shown that he *cannot* examine all the evidence pertaining to the question of God's character.

3) He should not therefore claim that his perspective is correct for he cannot be sure of his position regarding God.

Positions Claiming Total Uncertainty

"We cannot know whether God exists or not."

1) The believer must show the non-Christian that though his position may seem safe and neutral on the surface, it is actually a bold statement about God and His world. He is claiming that God has not made Himself known in a way that should be accepted by all men.

2) The believer may then explain that the unbeliever has not searched everywhere to see if there is any clear evidence for God. Moreover, he should point out that he cannot do so.

3) The non-Christian cannot be sure about his agnosticism.

"God's existence is a personal matter and should not be debated."

1) The Christian must see and demonstrate how such unbelievers are saying that there is enough evidence to know that belief in God must be entirely personal.

2) Yet, the Christian must also reveal how the non-Christian has not seen and cannot see enough evidence to know this for certain. On the back side of the moon, for instance, there may be convincing evidence that God does exist and that it is not a matter of personal belief.

3) The non-Christian cannot therefore be certain about his position and his objection is not valid.

Step 3: This basic approach for defending the existence of God then leads to the issue of greatest importance. The unbeliever is in the frustrating position we have shown him to be in because of his allegiance to independence. He has no right to sit as judge of God's existence; he must turn in faith to Christ and be saved from his hopeless state.

2. The Problem of Evil

Another difficulty for unbelievers which often rises in conversations is the problem of evil. If God is good and God created all things, then there must be something wrong with the Christian concept of God since there is evil in the world. Care must be taken to have a biblical perspective on the matter and present that perspective to the non-Christian.

a. Argument by Truth

Step 1: The believer should admit that he is going to approach this matter from a Christian point of view.

Step 2: There are many approaches to the biblical answer for this problem. We shall cite only a few.

Evidence from Scripture

1) God created the world good but man cast it into evil by his rebellion against God (Gen. 1:27; 3:17). Moreover, in line with His character God gives only good and perfect gifts (James 1:17).

2) Beyond this, men suffer even worse evil because God's program for His creation insists that men reap what they sow (Gal. 6:7).

3) Evil fits into God's overall plan of self-glorification as that which He will defeat and conquer (Ps. 110:1).

4) God never tempts men to sin, even when He tests their faithfulness to Him (James 1:13).

5) What God does is good, however, not because His activities pass human standards for goodness. God is good because He is God. Whatever He does with His creation is good and holy (James 1:13).

Evidence from the External World

6) God continues to order His universe for man's benefit (cf. Gen. 8:22).

7) God constantly gives good gifts to the world (James 1:17).

8) Even the fact that God allows us to continue to live shows His goodness toward us, for we all deserve to die (Rom. 3:23).

Evidence from Personal Experience

9) Believers in Christ know from their personal encounter with Christ that the existence of evil in the world does not give cause for calling the goodness of God into question. Believers know God's goodness as he has given them life in His Son.

Step 3: Demonstrate the allegiance of the non-Christian to independence and explain that his rejection of this perspective is because of this commitment.

b. Argument by Folly

The argument by folly will seek to show that non-Christian solutions to the problem of evil are inadequate.

Step 1: Show the unbeliever that his commitment has no solid ground beneath it.

Step 2: The specific stance which the unbeliever takes is self-refuting.

Positions Claiming Absolute Certainty

"God is evil."

1) The Christian must challenge this view by pointing out how the non-Christian has not fathomed and cannot fathom the motives and secret purposes of God's mind.

2) Because of these great limitations the non-Christian may not claim that God is evil simply because there is evil in the world.

"Since there is evil in the world, God must not exist."

1) This position may be shown to be inadequate by pointing out that the unbeliever has not heard and cannot hope to hear every explanation of the relation of God and evil.

2) He cannot be absolutely certain that there is no way for evil to exist in the creation of a good God.

Positions Claiming Total Uncertainty

"God's character and existence are confusing and show the senselessness of religious speculation."

1) The Christian should show that this position is not neutral. It is a very definite stance against Christianity.

2) Moreover, the fact that such non-Christians have not experienced and cannot experience all the evidence for the character and existence of God demonstrates that they cannot insist on silence in religious questions.

Step 3: The unbeliever should be told that his futility of thought stems from his commitment to independence and that he needs to forsake that commitment for faith in Christ.

B. Objections About Christ

There are many points of conflict between Christians and non-Christians which revolve around the person and work of Christ. Needless to say, we can only comment on a few of these issues. So, we will deal with the two items which arise most often.

1. The Deity of Christ

In our day it is very popular to believe that Jesus lived and taught in the past but to reject His claim to deity and to think of Him as a mere man. The Christian position is often ridiculed because it holds tenaciously to the true humanity and deity of Jesus.

a. Argument by Truth

Step 1: The believer should admit that his reasons for belief in the deity of Christ rest on his allegiance to Christ and His Word.

Step 2: The Christian evidences for Christ's divinity are numerous.

Evidence from Scripture

1) Jesus is called "God" throughout the New Testament (II Pet. 1:1; Tit. 2:13; I John 5:20; John 10:30; 20:28; 1:1). Thus He is made separate from all creatures.

2) Jesus Himself claimed to be the Lord of the Old Testament when he said, "before Abraham was born, I AM" (John 8:58).

3) Even the Old Testament spoke of the Messiah to come as "God with us" (Isa. 7:14) and "mighty God" (Isa. 9:16).

4) If Jesus were not God but merely a creature, then salvation would be brought about by a creature rather than by God alone.

Evidence from the External World

5) Jesus' position of kingship over the external world and His infallible control of all events demonstrate His true divinity.

6) The dramatic impact which Jesus' life had and has on the course of history demonstrates his divinity.

Evidence from Personal Experience

7) When men and women come to trust in Christ for salvation they meet Him and know Him not as a creature but as their Lord and God (cf. John 20:28).

Step 3: Point out to the unbeliever that he cannot see the truth of these arguments because of his religious commitment to independence.

b. Argument by Folly

To argue by folly is to show the non-Christian that he has no alternative acceptable to his own standards.

Step 1: Show the non-Christian that he cannot hope to support his commitment to independence upon which all his arguments against the divinity of Christ rest.

Step 2: The specific position which the non-Christian may take also leaves him without hope for truth.

Positions Claiming Absolute Certainty

"It is impossible for Jesus to be God and man."

1) The believer must show the non-Christian that his objection is not able to be supported. He does not have the sort of

knowledge of the universe, much less of God, necessary to make such a statement with certainty.

2) Who is this man, who has not seen and *cannot* see Jesus, to test His claim to divinity? Can a mere man decide what is possible and impossible for God?

3) If God is the Creator of all that is possible then surely He could become a man if He wished to do so.

"Jesus was just a good man."

1) The believer may show the poverty of this position by challenging the expertise of the non-Christian in this area. He certainly cannot support his position with historical evidence, except that which he greatly misconstrues.

2) The unbeliever should recognize that he cannot collect enough relevant evidence to hold his position.

"Jesus was a son of God as every human being is a son of God."

1) The unbeliever has not experienced and cannot experience enough to know for certain that man is partly created and partly divine. There is plenty of evidence to the contrary.

2) The unbeliever is especially unable to substantiate the idea that Jesus was merely the son of God as every human being. He never claimed this was so. He is clearly distinguished as the only begotten Son by Scripture. There is no support for this view of unbelief.

Positions Claiming Total Uncertainty

"We cannot know whether Jesus even claimed to be God much less whether He truly was."

1) This view should be shown to be making bold assertions about the reliability of Scripture and of the historical evidences.

2) The unbeliever should recognize that he cannot show enough relevant evidence to support his position.

Step 3: The non-Christian should be shown that the futility of his position stems from his commitment to independence. He must forsake that allegiance for faith in Christ.

2. The Resurrection of Christ

In the early days of the gospel a point of contention in many cases was the teaching that Christ had been raised from the dead. The resurrection is of vital importance to the Christian faith for without it there would be no transition from death to life for anyone. Consequently, the resurrection is a belief which we must be prepared to defend.

a. Argument by Truth

Step 1: The Christian should confess that his belief in the resurrection of Christ is a fundamental aspect of his religious commitment.

Step 2: There is ample support for the fact that Jesus was resurrected.

Evidence from Scripture

1) All the gospels record the resurrection as the declaration of Christ as the King and Savior.

2) Paul records the testimonies of eyewitnesses of the resurrected Christ and considers it a pillar of Christian belief (I Cor. 15:1-24).

3) Jesus predicted it (Matt. 16:21).

4) The Old Testament predicted the resurrection (Acts 2:25-36; Isa. 53:10-12; Ps. 16:10).

Evidence from the External World

5) The change from defeat to enthusiasm among the apostles can be accounted for only by the resurrection.

6) The testimony of the eyewitnesses as historical data gives great proof of the resurrection.

Evidence from Personal Experience

7) There are many in the world who know that Jesus was resurrected because they know His living presence in them.

Step 3: The Christian should demonstrate that the reason these arguments do not convince the unbeliever is that he is committed to independence.

a. Argument by Folly

Step 1: The unbeliever must be shown that commitment to independence cannot be justified. It is without solid ground beneath it.

Step 2: The specific objections raised by the non-Christian are futile and self-defeating also.

Positions Claiming Absolute Certainty

"Jesus was not dead on the cross; He never was resurrected."

1) The unbeliever cannot supply the evidence necessary to support this objection.

2) The biblical record makes it clear again and again that Jesus was dead (Matt. 15:44–45).

3) The unbeliever is unable to have a supported objection.

"Jesus' resurrection is a myth created by the apostles."

1) The unbeliever cannot support his view with conclusive evidence.

2) His view is merely speculative.

"It is impossible for someone who is dead to be alive again."

1) The believer may point out the many things in the world for which there is no thorough scientific explanation.

2) The scientific method, on which the non-Christian's objection is based, cannot be established as the standard for truth.

3) If God does exist, why would it be so impossible for Him to raise someone from the dead?

4) The unbeliever has not experienced enough evidence to know that it is impossible for Jesus to have been raised.

Positions Claiming Total Uncertainty

"There is reason to doubt the resurrection, though we cannot be sure."

1) The believer should show the non-Christian that his stance is conclusively opposed to Christianity, for to question the resurrection even for a moment is to reject Christ.

2) The non-Christian cannot experience enough evidence to be sure that the evidence does cast doubt on the resurrection of Christ.

3) There is no reason to even doubt the resurrection.

Step 3: The unbeliever cannot object to the certainty of Christ's resurrection without betraying himself for he is in need of salvation.

Review Questions:

1. What are the three basic steps in the argument by truth? Argument by folly?
2. How would you argue by truth for:
   a. the existence of God?
   b. the goodness of God?
   c. the deity of Christ?
   d. the resurrection of Christ?
3. How would you argue by folly to these responses?
   a. "We can't be sure that God exists."
   b. "There is no God."
   c. "There is too much evil in the world for God to exist."
   d. "It is impossible for Jesus to be God and man."
   e. "The dead are not able to be alive again."

Lesson 12: Defending the Faith (2)

The specific objections raised against the Christian position are numerous and far reaching. In this lesson we will continue to deal with responses to some of the typical objections offered by unbelievers.

A. Objections about the Bible

In most evangelistic and apologetic conversations with unbelievers the authority of the Bible becomes a central issue. If the argument by truth is employed by the Christian with any regularity, it becomes apparent to the unbeliever that the Christian seeks his answers to life's questions from the Bible. The believer does not question its reliability. Instead, he regards the Bible as the very Word of God.

1. The Authority of the Bible

Though in some cases even unbelievers may give formal assent or surface agreement with the Christian view of biblical authority, very often the defender of the faith is asked, "Why do you accept the Bible as the Word of God, and why should I accept it?" The Christian must be prepared to answer this question.

a. Argument by Truth

Step 1: The believer should admit that his belief in Scripture as God's Word rests on his commitment to Christ.

Step 2: The Christian evidence for believing the Bible to be God's Word should be given.

Evidences from Scripture

1) The Scriptures are inspired by God in such a way as to be authoritative in all that they say (II Tim. 3:14–17).

2) The necessity of belief in this written Word of God is also made clear (I Cor. 14:37; John 5:47; Luke 16:31; I John 4:6).

3) God has promised to preserve His Word for His people in all generations (Matt. 5:17; John 10:31; Isa. 59:21; Ps. 111:7, 8).

4) The New Testament writers always appealed to the Old Testament as an infallible and authoritative guide.

5) The New Testament claims the same authority for itself as it recognizes in the Old Testament (I Tim. 5:18; II Pet. 3:16).

6) As Christians we receive the Bible as the Word of God which cannot be judged by any higher standard. The Word of God speaks for itself; it is not verified by any other than the self-verifying Father, Son, and Holy Spirit.

7) From the Christian perspective any apparent difficulties with the teaching of the Bible rest on our misunderstanding the world, the Bible, or both. The problem is not in the Bible itself.

8) We can have confidence that the Holy Spirit of God is teaching us as we earnestly seek to understand the Bible. Though we may be unclear on some matters there are many portions of Scripture which are made obviously clear by God's Spirit.

Evidence from the External World

9) Throughout the centuries the Bible has played a formative role in Western society.

10) The text of the Old and New Testaments have been preserved through history with great accuracy.

11) There has never been a proven contradiction between what the Bible says and the reality of the world. In fact, again and again the Bible is confirmed by scientific investigation.

Evidence from Personal Experience

12) Christians accept the Bible as the Word of God because of the Holy Spirit's testimony to their hearts that the Bible's own claim is true.

13) When we trust Christ through the message of the gospel we begin to hear the voice of God in the Bible and to obey. As we grow in the faith that testimony of the Spirit is confirmed again and again.

14) Of course, we know the testimony of the Spirit by receiving Christ whom the Father sent and we know the Father, Christ, and the Holy Spirit by the testimony of Scripture. These testify to themselves and to each other.

Step 3: The unbeliever should be shown that he does not accept these arguments because he is committed to independence.

b. Argument by Folly

Step 1: The unbeliever should be shown that his rejection of the authority of Scripture rests on the assumption of his own authority which cannot be justified.

Step 2: The specific ways in which non-Christians object to the authority of Scripture may be shown to be self-defeating as well.

Positions Claiming Absolute Certainty

"The Bible contradicts itself."

1) The unbeliever has not examined the Bible and other resource materials enough to know that he has not simply misunderstood a passage which he thinks is contradictory. It is often the case that non-Christians call passages contradictory when just a little reflection shows them to be quite harmonious.

2) The unbeliever cannot examine the Bible and other resource materials enough to know that he has exhausted all the possible explanations of his so-called contradiction.

3) Until he can say with absolute certainty that there are contradictions in the Bible he cannot reject biblical authority on this basis.

"The Bible contradicts history."

1) No non-Christian has dealt with biblical archeology and history enough to know for certain that he has not misunderstood the historical research or the Bible. There are plenty of examples

where earlier research pointed to discrepancies between the Bible and actual history which have now been shown to be mistakes in historical research.

2) It is impossible for the historian to know for certain that his understanding of archeological discoveries is correct. He has not explored all the possible interpretations of his discoveries.

3) Since certainty in these matters is impossible to find, it is impossible for the unbeliever to reject the Bible with certainty.

"The Bible is not God's Word for it was written by men."

1) The unbeliever has not established and cannot establish with certainty that the humanity of the Bible necessarily means there are errors in the Bible. He cannot rule out with certainty the divine protection of inspiration which the Christian claims.

2) The non-Christian has no way to prove that he can reject the authority of Scripture because it was written by humans.

"The Bible is terribly mythological and unscientific."

1) The non-Christian has not examined and cannot examine the question of the reality of miracles enough to know that they are impossible. For all he knows they might have actually occurred as recorded.

2) To deny the reality of miracles would require a complete analysis of every claim of miracles and a complete explanation of every other event that has ever occurred in the universe. Both of these requirements are impossible and therefore the certain rejection of the Bible on this basis is impossible.

Positions Claiming Total Uncertainty

"The Bible is too ambiguous."

1) The non-Christian must be shown that he has not actually dealt with the problem of interpreting the Bible thoroughly enough. Any piece of literature can be interpreted in a number of ways. Yet, that does not alter the fact that the literature has a definite message. For instance, it may be said that Mary's lamb of the favorite nursery rhyme was not "little." Perhaps Mary was extremely large. The poem is open to that sort of interpretation, but the interpretation clearly contradicts the true meaning of the poem. The same is true of many interpretations of the Bible.

2) The non-Christian cannot be sure that true understanding of the Bible is impossible until he himself has examined every interpretation ever offered. It may very well be that the Holy Spirit does relate the truth of Scripture as the believer claims. The non-Christian cannot disprove that claim.

"The original Bible has been lost through the centuries."

1) The non-Christian must be shown that he has not examined all the manuscript evidence which does exist today. He is incapable of discrediting the science of textual criticism. He is therefore unable to reject the authority of the Bible on the assumption that the text has been lost. There is plenty of evidence to the contrary.

2) The unbeliever is unable to have the certainty regarding the text of the Bible necessary to disprove the promises of God for the preservation of Scripture.

2. Other Religious Books

Very often non-Christians argue against the idea that the Bible is God's Word by pointing to the fact that the Koran, the Book of Mormon, etc. also claim to be God's Word. The Christian is usually accused of being arbitrary or unfairly biased in his choice of the Bible because all of these and other books claim religious authority. In one way or another he will ask, "Why don't you accept all the books of other religions which claim to be divinely inspired?"

a. Argument by Truth

Step 1: The Christian should admit that even his answer to this question will necessarily rest on his commitment to Christ.

Step 2: There are several lines of argument for the Christian view on the uniqueness of the Bible.

Evidence from Scripture

1) The Bible warns against false prophets who will claim to be from God (Matt. 24:24). It even warns against counterfeit Scripture (II Thess. 3:17). The Christian must be committed to evaluating these and other voices by the voice of the Bible.

Evidence from the External World

2) Christianity is a religion which has its roots in Judaism and in Jesus of Nazareth. As a Jew, Jesus accepted the Old Testament as the Word of God. As the Messiah of the new age He commissioned His apostles to oversee the production of the New Testament. As Jesus is uniquely God, the Bible is uniquely God's Word.

Evidence from Personal Experience

3) It was not that the Christian chose the Scriptures of the Old and New Testaments independently. He was convinced by God Himself to believe the Bible, even as the unbeliever will be convinced if he will but trust in Christ.

Step 3: The unbeliever should be shown that these arguments by truth are not compelling because of his commitment to independence from God.

b. Argument by Folly

Step 1: The believer should show the unbeliever that his objection is based on a groundless commitment and is therefore without weight.

Step 2: It is often beneficial to challenge the particular stance of the unbeliever with regard to this issue.

Positions Claiming Absolute Certainty

"No religious books have any authority."

1) Show the unbeliever that he has not examined the many factors that enter into a question of this nature. He is no expert on every religion of the world. He cannot know all there is to know even about the Bible much less every other book which claims authority.

2) Since the non-Christian is so limited he simply cannot reject the uniqueness of the Bible.

"Only my religious book has authority."

1) The unbeliever may be a member of one of many cults which have their own religious books. Whatever the case, the non-

Christian has not searched all the religions of the world and he cannot.

2) For this reason the unbeliever who rests his faith on independence from the true God cannot be sure of the authority of his religious book.

Positions Claiming Total Uncertainty

"I don't believe we should say one religious book is better than another."

1) Such unbelievers usually try to be neutral and generous to religious people. The Christian, however, must show them that they have no solid basis for their view. They have not experienced all that would be necessary to show that one book is no better than another.

2) The non-Christian cannot reject the uniqueness of biblical revelation in this way for there is no way of supporting his own view.

Step 3: The Christian should demonstrate to the unbeliever that his positions are futile because of his commitment to independence. The only way of escaping this expression of God's judgment is by repentance and faith in Christ.

We have not covered all the possible objections raised by disbelief against the Bible. Nevertheless, the most important issues have been dealt with, and the apologist should be able to defend the Christian position on these matters.

B. Objections About Man

Another category into which we may group the typical objections unbelievers raise against the Christian position are questions about the Christian view of man. We shall deal with three of the most basic questions.

1. The Sinfulness of Man

The Christian doctrine of sin and judgment often causes objections to be raised by the unbeliever. In one way or another he may say, "Why should I believe in the sinfulness of man?"

a. Argument by Truth

Step 1: The believer should confess that his view of the sinfulness of man is based on his commitment to Christ as his Lord and Saviour.

Step 2: The Christian evidence for the position is obvious.

Evidence from Scripture

1) The Bible teaches that all have sinned in Adam (Rom. 5:12f.).

2) All men have also sinned personally by breaking God's Law (Rom. 3:23).

3) Even those who have never heard of the Christian gospel have sinned and are therefore under God's judgment (Rom. 1:18f.).

Evidence from the External World

4) If we consider the history of mankind, it is not difficult to see the affects of sin. History is marked by its wars, murders, violence and hatred. Though no man is as evil as he could be and some are better than others, all men are rebels against God.

Evidence from Personal Experience

5) Every Christian knows from his conversion experience that man is indeed sinful.

Step 3: The unbeliever should be told that these evidences do not hold much weight for him because of his commitment to independence.

b. Argument by Folly

Step 1: The commitment to independence should be shown to be groundless.

Step 2: The specific objections which non-Christians take are futile attempts at the denial of truth.

Positions Claiming Absolute Certainty

"I think all people are good at heart."

1) The unbeliever must be shown that he has not dealt with all the evidence for man's character. There are numerous examples of the evils of men.

2) Show the unbeliever that he cannot know the heart of man well enough to say for certain that he is basically good.

3) The unbeliever cannot reject the Christian view on this basis because he cannot be certain about his own view.

"Some people are good and others are bad."

1) The Christian should show the unbeliever that his view cannot be supported because he cannot know the universe well enough to decide independently between good and bad people.

2) In order to make such a claim, the unbeliever must assume the sort of absolute certainty which he cannot have because of his refusal to submit himself to God.

Positions Claiming Total Uncertainty

"It is the height of arrogance to say that anyone is evil."

1) The Christian should show the unbeliever that his view is not neutral and uncommitted. He has made a very definite and unbending statement.

2) The unbeliever cannot say with certainty that we should not make judgments about the character of men. He is unable to gather enough evidence to support his view.

Step 3: The non-Christian should be challenged to forsake his commitment for faith in Christ.

2. The Responsibility of Man

Another issue that is often brought up by non-Christians regards the relation of divine sovereignty and human responsibility. "If God is in control of things then the evil in the world is His fault, not man's," the unbeliever may say.

a. Argument by Truth

Step 1: The Christian's position stems from his commitment to Christ.

Step 2: The biblical answer to this issue is simple and straightforward, though often misunderstood.

Evidence from Scripture

1) God is in control of everything, working all for His own purpose and glory (Rom. 11:36; Eph. 1:11).

2) As the Creator of all, God is the rightful judge of man.

3) At the same time man has truly sinned by breaking the Law of God, and God pronounces judgment on all law-breakers (Rom. 2:12).

4) God's justice and wisdom in these matters are not to be called into question by His creatures (Rom. 9:19–21).

5) God's control of things is not contrary to the responsibility of man. It is the very foundation of it. If God were not in control He could not hold man responsible. Man is accountable to God *because* God is sovereign; he should obey God *because* God is in control of things. Moreover, man has significance *because* God has sovereignly ordained significance for man. Whatever responsibility we have is *founded* on God's sovereignty, not in spite of it. Without God's sovereignty man would have no responsibility (cf. Phil. 2:12, 13).

Evidence from the External World

6) History shows plainly both the sovereignty of God as He controls and works all things toward consummation in Christ. Yet, the role of human agency is clearly discernible as well in the great and small figures of history.

Evidence from Personal Experience

7) The believer knows the reality of responsibility based on sovereignty. His relationship with God is one of submission to His Lordship and conformity to His will. Without sovereignty and responsibility, such a perspective would be impossible.

Step 3: Establish that the non-Christian does not accept this view because of his commitment to independence.

b. Argument by Folly

Step 1: The unbeliever's commitment to independence is unable to be supported.

Step 2: The positions which are taken by the non-Christian can be refuted on their own ground.

Positions Claiming Absolute Certainty

"God is unfair if He holds us guilty."

1) The Christian should show the unbeliever that he has not examined every explanation of God's justice and fairness. In fact there may be an explanation but one unavailable to him. He cannot, therefore, be sure of his view.

2) The unbeliever is hardly in a position of being able to judge the fairness and justice of God. He cannot be certain about things in this world, much less the things of God.

"A loving God would not hold man guilty."

1) The unbeliever cannot know that God's love contradicts His holding man responsible.

Step 3: The unbeliever should be challenged to forsake his commitment to independence.

Whatever the case may be, non-Christians have no grounds upon which they may make a valid objection to the Christian view of God's sovereignty and man's responsibility.

In this lesson we have observed some of the lines of argument involving the Christian view of the Bible and man. These are, to be sure, only a sampling of the possible directions which could be taken. If, however, the Christian will keep in mind the basic structure of the Christian responses given here it will not be difficult to handle most objections which can be raised.

Review Questions:

1. What are the three steps in the argument by truth? Argument by folly?
2. How would you argue by truth for:
   a. the Bible as the Word of God?
   b. the uniqueness of the Bible in distinction from other religious books?
   c. the sinfulness of all men?
   d. the sovereignty of God and human responsibility?
3. How would you argue by folly against these objections?
   a. "The Bible contradicts itself."
   b. "The Bible contradicts history."
   c. "The Bible is not the Word of God because it was written by men."
   d. "The Bible is too mythological to be God's Word.
   e. "The Bible is too ambiguous to be God's Word."
   f. "The Bible has been lost through translation and transmission."
   g. "There are so many religious books that the Bible is not unique."
   h. "No religious books can have God's authority."
   i. "Only my religious book has authority."
   j. "We should not say one religious book is better than another."
   k. "I think all people are good at heart."
   l. "Some people are good and others are bad."
   m. "I don't think we should be so arrogant as to think anyone is evil."
   n. "God is unfair if He holds us guilty."
   o. "A loving God would not hold men guilty."

Lesson 13. Defending the Faith (3)

In the last lesson we saw how to defend the Christian position against common objections which are often raised by unbelievers. Issues involving the world and the need of faith are seldom ignored by unbelievers. We shall deal with each of these in some detail.

A. Objections About the World

The origin and destiny of the world are matters of concern to most people. Christianity has a very definite perspective which must be defended thoroughly. In these matters unbelievers generally know very little even by their own standards; nevertheless they are not prepared to accept the Christian view.

1. The Origin of the World

The biblical doctrine of creation is of central importance to the Christian faith. Yet, since the time of Charles Darwin various forms of evolutionary theories have been major tenets of scientific thought. As a result, a point of conflict between the Christian and non-Christian today is often the question of creation and evolution. In one way or another the unbeliever will object saying, "Why should I believe in Christ when evolution has been proven true?"

a. Argument by Truth

Step 1: The Christian should admit that his perspective on the question of creation stems from his commitment to Christ.

Step 2: The Christian position on creation is radically opposed to many of the evolutionary theories popular today. It is difficult to take a stand on all the issues involved but there are certain ideas to which every Christian should hold without hesitation or compromise. For these issues we must present the Christian evidence.

Evidence from Scripture

1) God created the world. The universe did not come into being by chance (Gen. 1:1).

2) The order of the world is established and upheld by God (Gen.1:2f.). Whatever process may have occurred was not random; God was fully in control.

3) There is an obvious distinction between human beings, the image of God, and animals, both in origin (Gen. 1:24, 25; 2:7) and in their relationship to each other (Gen. 1:26-30; 2:20-23). Man does not have a common biological ancestor with the animals.

4) True science, the pursuit of true knowledge, will never reject the Bible in the face of "scientific evidence." It will always hold firm the absolute authority of the Bible and interpret scientific evidence which seems contrary to the Bible in the light of the Bible.

5) What similarities there are between different living creatures does not point to common ancestry but to a common Creator. As an artist's various paintings resemble one another, so God's various works resemble one another because of divine creation.

Evidence from the External World

6) Many respectable scientists who are Christians take the same scientific evidence used to prove evolution and arrive at other conclusions.

7) The evidence for evolution is far from conclusive.

Evidence from Personal Experience

8) The believer who knows his God realizes that he is not a mere animal. He is the image of God.

9) The believer also knows personally that it is God who is in control of things, not chance.

Step 3: The Christian should point out that these arguments have no weight with the unbeliever because of his commitment to independence.

b. Argument by Folly

Step 1: The non-Christian should be shown the groundlessness of commitment to independence.

Step 2: There are many approaches which can be used when answering the unbeliever on the issue of evolution. We shall present a few of these.

1) Show the unbeliever that he has not dealt adequately with all the evidence for and against evolution.

a) Criticize the reliability of science in general in matters such as these.

b) Point out that scientists who believe in evolution believe all sorts of things which cannot be proven scientifically (e.g., the world is controlled by chance; similarity proves common ancestry).

c) Show the unbeliever that non-Christian scientists are yet to give an adequate explanation for the lack of fossil evidence for the successive stages of the supposed evolutionary scale.

2) Moreover, the Christian should remind the unbeliever that scientists cannot examine all the evidence and may someday change their views as they have before. It is for this reason that evolution is still called a *theory* even by its advocates and this is why there are many differing evolutionary theories.

3) The unbeliever cannot object with certainty against the Christian position because his own view is so totally uncertain.

Step 3: Challenge the non-Christian concerning his commitment to independence.

2. The End of the World

Along with objections about the beginning of the world, unbelievers also reject the Christian view of the end of the world.

Many times non-Christians scoff at Christianity saying, "Why should I believe there will someday be a judgment?"

a. Argument by Truth

Step 1: The Christian's view of the end of the world is determined by his commitment to Christ.

Step 2: There are many lines of argument by truth for the coming judgment. We shall mention only two.

Evidence from Scripture

1) The Bible declares explicitly that there is a judgment to come (Matt. 25:1ff.; Heb. 9:27).

2) The Bible gives numerous examples of times when God punished people as a foretaste of the coming judgment.

Evidence from the External World

3) The world system is moving toward a consummation of blessing and judgment.

Evidence from Personal Experience

4) The believer came to grips with the reality of future judgment when he first trusted Christ.

Step 3: The reason these evidences are not convincing to the non-Christian is that he is committed to independence.

b. Argument by Folly

Step 1: The commitment to independence is not able to be supported.

Step 2: The specific counter-position of the non-Christian must be shown to be futile and self-defeating.

Positions Claiming Absolute Certainty

"There is no judgment because there is no afterlife."

1) The unbeliever has not dealt with all the evidence for and against the idea of an afterlife, especially in light of recent non-

Christian discoveries in this area by those who have been near death and later revived.

2) The unbeliever is only guessing that there is no afterlife. He has not died and is unable to examine all the issues and evidence regarding it.

"There is no judgment because humans are going through hell in this life."

1) The unbeliever should be shown that he cannot supply evidence necessary to hold his view with certainty.

2) Moreover, he is in no position to determine from his limited perspective what sort of punishment unbelief deserves.

"There is no judgment, only the inevitable natural disaster coming from war, pollution, or overpopulation."

1) The unbeliever has not experienced enough to reject with certainty that God is in control of the world in such a way as to keep world-wide destruction from occurring.

2) Even if the non-Christian were correct, his view does not rule out the Christian view.

"There is no judgment, for man is going to reach utopia."

1) Point out that the unbeliever has nothing but blind faith that this is true. He can have no certainty of such things.

2) Remind the unbeliever of the evidence of man's sinfulness which is contrary to the idea of a utopia.

3) Show the non-Christian that he cannot have certainty about these things because he cannot experience them fully.

Positions Claiming Total Uncertainty

"It is not possible to know about events beyond the grave."

1) The unbeliever should be shown that he is not remaining silent with regard to the nature of things after death. He is asserting his position with absolute certainty.

2) The non-Christian cannot make this statement if it is true. If we can know nothing about afterlife we cannot know that we can know nothing.

It is evident that non-Christians do not have any ground upon which to object to the Christian concept of a future judgment. Only the Christian view is defensible.

B. Objections About the Need for Faith

The Christian gospel is a message which demands faith from unbelievers. On the one hand, Christian faith insists on the sure conviction of commitment to those truths revealed by God. We are to be dependently certain beyond doubt of what God has said. On the other hand, Christian faith demands recognition of our limitations and humble trust in God for those things which have not been revealed or which we do not understand. Christians recognize that the Creator-creature distinction causes them to be dependently uncertain. The gospel therefore demands both certainty and uncertainty in a harmonious relationship. As a result, the need for faith is often objected to by non-Christians for they are torn between their own forms of absolute certainty and total uncertainty. Due to their rejection of God, they can have no confidence in man's ability to know. This dilemma is inescapable. Nevertheless, one way in which non-Christians seek to account for this difficulty is to claim either certainty or uncertainty by ignoring the opposite conviction. Consequently, non-Christians may object to the Christian view of faith in two ways: 1) Claiming to be absolutely certain, they will object to Christian uncertainty. 2) Claiming that man must be totally uncertain, they will object to Christian certainty. We shall deal with each of these objections for they form the basic direction of every denial of Christian truth.

1. Christian Uncertainty

There are any number of ways in which unbelievers question Christian uncertainty from the stance of their own certainty. Usually, the unbeliever will think of faith as unreasonable and unacceptable intellectually. He is convinced that he cannot accept Christianity because there are too many things that he would have to take *by faith*. If Christianity did not demand an acceptance of things beyond our comprehension and beyond logical reasoning, he would become a Christian. Yet, until then he will ask, "Why should I accept Christianity? Faith is too naive."

a. Argument by Truth

Step 1: The Christian should admit that his view of faith stems from his commitment to Christ.

Step 2: The argument by truth against this sort of objection is the presentation of the Christian view of uncertainty.

Evidence from Scripture

1) Some things are hidden from man (Deut. 29:29).

2) God alone knows all things (Ps. 33:13–15; 139:2–12; 147:5; II Chron. 16:9; Jer. 17:10).

3) God can and must be trusted in those matters He has revealed which may seem unexplained and unsupported by human wisdom. Moreover, those things unknown to us are fully known to God and we may trust His ability to understand correctly.

Evidence from the External World

4) The history of man's quest for knowledge has numerous examples of how his limitedness makes man unable to have comprehensive knowledge and thereby reveals man's need for the all-knowing God of Scripture.

Evidence from Personal Experience

5) When men and women become Christians they are made aware of their inability to know all things and their need to trust God in those things which are unknown.

Step 3: The unbeliever should be shown that he does not accept these evidences because of his commitment to independence.

b. Argument by Folly

Step 1: The unbeliever's commitment should be exposed as groundless.

Step 2: The argument by folly should show the unbeliever that his view of faith is self-contradictory.

1) The unbeliever should be shown that he cannot know all things so he must have blind faith in himself in order to object in this fashion to Christianity.

2) The unbeliever's insistence *against faith* is itself based on a *faith* assumption.

3) The unbeliever objects to his own view if he objects to Christianity because it demands faith. In fact, because the Christian faith rests on God, and is not blind but sure, the unbeliever's objection applies only to his own position of blind faith.

Step 3: The non-Christian should be challenged to forsake his commitment to independence.

2. Christian Certainty

Non-Christians will often also object to the Christian demand for faith from their position of total uncertainty. In such cases, the unbeliever refuses to believe in Christ because there are too many things that he would have to believe for certain. He is convinced that there is no way of being sure of the doctrines of faith. Basically the unbeliever will object saying, "You're too dogmatic."

a. Argument by Truth

Step 1: The Christian should admit that his views stem from his basic commitment.

Step 2: There are several basic arguments appropriate in this case.

Evidence from Scripture

1) God has revealed Himself in Scripture (II Tim. 3:16).

2) Christ claimed exclusive mediation to the Father (John 14:6).

3) God's truth abides forever (I Pet. 1:24–25).

4) What God has spoken is to be received as infallibly authoritative (Deut. 29:29).

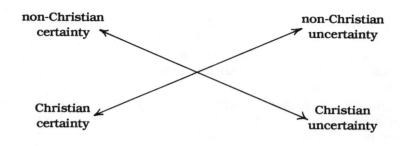

non-Christian
certainty

non-Christian
uncertainty

Christian
certainty

Christian
uncertainty

Figure 25

Evidence from the External World

5) The world is understandable to some extent even though it is not entirely understandable because of God's ordering and structuring of it.

Evidence from Personal Experience

6) The believer in Christ knows that what God has said is true and is to be received as absolutely authoritative.

Step 3: The unbeliever should be shown that his commitment to independence causes these arguments to be without weight in his eyes.

b. Argument by Folly

Step 1: Show that commitment to independence cannot be justified.

Step 2: The stance of the unbeliever is self-defeating and self-contradictory.

1) The unbeliever should be shown that he cannot produce enough evidence to know for sure that Christianity is too dogmatic.

2) The unbeliever is being as dogmatic as he is accusing the believer of being. Consequently, he is objecting to his own position.

3) The non-Christian is committed to a position of uncertainty, the certainty of which is founded on blind faith.

Step 3: The non-Christian should be challenged to forsake his commitment to independence which has thrown him into this dilemma.

Though non-Christians will object to the Christian faith from their perspectives of absolute certainty and total uncertainty, they nevertheless contradict their own views as they do so (see Fig. 25).

Review Questions:

1. What are the three steps in the argument by truth? Argument by folly?
2. How would you argue by truth for:
    a. the origin of the world?
    b. the end of the world?
    c. the certainty of faith?
    d. the uncertainty of faith?
3. How would you argue by folly against these objections?
    a. "Evolution disproves Christianity."
    b. "There is no judgment."
    c. "Christianity is too naive."
    d. "Christianity is too dogmatic."

Lesson 14. An Apologetic Parable

There was once a man by the name of Defenseless Denny. When he heard the gospel, he turned to Christ as his Lord and Saviour. Full of joy and full of zeal Denny visited his next door neighbors, Certain Cindy and David Doubter Nogod. Mr. and Mrs. Nogod were his closest friends before he became a Christian. As Denny approached the Nogod's front door he remembered the many evenings they spent together scoffing at all their Christian neighbors. Denny hoped that Cindy and David would come to know the new life in Christ which he had been given so freely. Certain Cindy and David Doubter had heard of Denny's new religion and as they welcomed him into their home they were determined to change his mind. Confrontation was inevitable; Denny tried to tell the Nogods of their need for salvation, but at every point Cindy and David would interrupt with objections.

"You don't really believe your religion is true, do you?" Cindy exclaimed. "This religious talk is ridiculous. You and I both know that Christianity is unscientific superstition. Come on now Denny! You can't expect me to believe something that isn't proven."

Denny was surprised. After all, he didn't have that much trouble when he heard the gospel. "Maybe it's just Certain Cindy's stubbornness,"Denny said to himself. But David Doubter didn't react much better to the claims of Christ.

"Look Denny, I know you're sincere and mean well but I just don't think we can be sure about religion. There are thousands of religions in the world. We can't decide that one is better than another," David said. "You sure have become arrogant saying that we have to believe in Jesus to be with God. You're too narrowminded. I try to be more humble than that."

David Doubter's response started Denny thinking. "Maybe I didn't look into Christianity close enough before I committed my life to Christ. Maybe I was too naive. Maybe I am too dogmatic." Defenseless Denny left the Nogods' discouraged and confused.

On the way home, Denny met one of his new Christian friends, Freddie Factfinder. Freddie was loaded down with six books in each arm; he always carried lots of books and paper. Freddie had quite a mind but as he always said, "You never know what new facts will be discovered." When Denny told him of his encounter with Cindy and David, Freddie was sympathetic. He, too, had shared the gospel with his friends and had been discouraged at their unbelief. "The problem with you," Freddie urged, "is that you just don't have enough ammunition to support your witness. You need *facts* to convince the unbeliever." Denny and Freddie talked for some time about evidences for Christianity. Freddie had found facts in all the sciences that give great weight to the Christian view of things. In fact, Freddie carried an ever-increasing list of facts that support Christianity. Defenseless Denny was thrilled by the confidence that Freddie had and invited him to go along on a return visit to the Nogod home.

The Nogods were glad to see Denny again and welcomed Freddie into their home. Freddie was introduced as "a Christian who knows the facts." This pleased both Cindy and David. Now they could better understand what Denny must be thinking.

"Denny tells me that you are not Christians," Freddie began. "Is there any particular reason why you won't believe in Christ? I have found plenty of facts which make Christianity reasonable."

Certain Cindy smiled and said, "Let's hear why you think I should believe there is a God."

Freddie reached for his list of evidences for God's existence and began reading them to Cindy. "1. Nearly everybody thinks there is a God of some sort. 2. The law of cause and effect shows that there must be a divine Cause for the world. 3. The order of the universe points to a God who designed it," Freddie read with confidence.

Certain Cindy pointed to a shelf of books across the room and said, "Don't you know that those old fashioned arguments were refuted long ago? You cannot establish God's existence simply because lots of people believe it. People have believed lots of things in the past which were later shown to be wrong. Besides that, who's to say the whole world had to have a divine Cause? The law of cause and effect is itself debatable and even so, logically it would point to a creaturely cause for the world, not a divine Cause. Moreover, the design of the world could have come about by chance or by the efforts of many gods, not just by your God! If you can't do any better than that, I'm afraid your facts are not too convincing, Freddie."

Somewhat dismayed, Freddie turned to David Doubter. "Freddie," David said, "I'm not as certain as Cindy but I do know that your arguments are not conclusive. It's awfully hard to know for sure whether God exists or not. I see evidence for it and against it; I think any honest person would have to remain silent on the question." Freddie was frustrated but not defeated.

"Let's assume, just for the sake of argument that there is a god," Freddie suggested.

Cindy and David agreed.

"I think that Jesus was God come in the flesh and that the Bible is God's Word," Freddie argued.

Cindy and David responded, "What sort of facts do you have to prove those claims?"

"Well," said Freddie, "Jesus claimed to be God and He was no lunatic or liar. So, He must have been God."

Cindy couldn't remain silent. "Look," urged Cindy. "I'm no lunatic and I'm not a liar but if I were convinced I were God and said so, that wouldn't prove that I was God. Besides, well known historians debate even whether Jesus ever lived, and if he did live, whether he actually claimed to be God at all. You can't prove that Jesus is God because He claimed to be. You've got to find better facts, Mr. Factfinder."

"What about the resurrection?" exclaimed Freddie. "Surely Jesus is shown to be God by the empty tomb!"

Cindy argued, "To begin with, it would take many more facts than you're able to produce to convince me that Jesus was resurrected. I'm certain there would be a better explanation for it than His divinity."

"I have to disagree with you again, Freddie," confessed David. "The myths of religions are so many and so unbelievable, it is impossible to know which ones are true."

Nearly desperate, Freddie demanded. "The Bible says all these things are true and I can prove that the Bible is trustworthy. There are no contradictions in the Bible. The Bible is proven true by historians and scientists. The Bible even claims to be God's Word."

"So what?" Cindy contended. "I think there are plenty of contradictions in the Bible. Show me the logic of saying that Jesus was a man and was God at the same time! Besides this, there are plenty of noted authorities who say there are clear differences between history, science and the Bible."

David Doubter concurred, "I'm sure you mean well but I'm afraid you haven't presented a convincing argument."

At that point Denny interrupted and said, "Why, Freddie Factfinder, you're as defenseless as I am. I thought you had it all figured out."

"I did too," replied Freddie. "I guess I've never run into unbelievers who could think so quickly. We need to go home and find some more facts that we can use."

"What's the use," Denny said. "You go and find your facts. They've been little help to me."

So they both said good-bye to the Nogods and went their separate ways.

The next day Defenseless Denny ran into his Christian neighbor Benny Bible Banger. After listening to the events of the last evening, Benny said, "I could have told you that would happen! Freddie Factfinder goes about things all wrong. You can never argue unbelievers into the faith. All we can do is preach the gospel and demand that they believe."

It was evident to Denny that Benny was at least partially right. All of Freddie's facts couldn't convince Cindy and David. "Maybe Benny is right. Maybe we should not try to defend the faith," Denny thought to himself. "Let's go visit the Nogods and see if your approach is better than Freddie's," Denny said. Benny agreed and the two set off for another confrontation.

"Cindy and David," Denny said. "I would like for you to meet my friend Benny Bible Banger."

By this time the Nogods were suspicious of Denny's Christian friends, but they did not wish to be rude.

"Come in and have a seat," David said reluctantly.

Benny began to share his faith in Christ with Cindy and David saying, "I want you to forget what Freddie Factfinder said to you yesterday. He was wrong for trying to prove Christianity to you with evidences. Christianity is not reasonable; it is a matter of faith." Benny continued, "The fact is that science and reason are of the devil. To know God you have to just believe what the Bible says by faith. If we try to think through the claims of Christ we will never know the truth."

"Why should I believe in the Bible?" Certain Cindy asked.

"You must believe because it is wrong not to believe the Bible," Benny replied.

"Do you mean that we have to give up thinking altogether?"

"Yes."

"I don't know about David, but I'm convinced that you Christians are just pulling at straws. You know as well as I that Christianity is ridiculous so you claim that thinking and reasoning about it is wrong. I will not believe in the Bible without some basis for belief," Cindy concluded.

"I'm afraid I have to go along with Cindy," David said. "If I can't reason about Christianity then how can I decide if it's right or wrong? From your perspective one religion could be just as true as another. I had a hard enough time with Freddie Factfinger, but I find your view impossible to accept."

Disappointed once again, Denny took Benny by the arm and grumbled, "Come on, Benny, let's go home!"

Later that day, Defenseless Denny saw Chris Christian. It wasn't long before the Nogods became a topic of discussion between them as well.

"You know, Chris," Denny confessed. "I was really disappointed to learn that the Christian faith cannot be defended."

"Wait a minute," Chris interrupted. "Christianity can be defended. It's just that Freddie and Benny don't know how to defend their faith. The Bible commands us to 'make a defense to everyone who asks . . .' (I Pet. 3:15)."

"I know that I believe in Christ, but Cindy and David were able to destroy Freddie's and Benny's arguments," Denny remarked.

"Yes, I know brother Freddie and brother Benny. They mean well and try hard, but they are not biblical in their approach. I'm not guaranteeing that Cindy and David will become believers, but I can promise that a biblical approach will give them plenty of reason to accept the Christian view. Moreover, it will encourage you and strengthen your faith," she said sincerely.

"Chris, I have a hard time believing you, but I guess I can give your way a fair chance, too. What's your approach?" Denny asked.

Chris Christian went on to explain to Denny what a biblical defense was like and how it would work out in different conversations. "The first thing you have to realize," she told Denny, "is that both Freddie and Benny had some correct notions about defending the faith. Freddie is right when he insists that Christianity can be defended rationally. Reasoning with the unbeliever is an important part of a biblical defense. On the other hand, Benny has made an important point. He bangs the Bible because man should never act as the judge of God's Word. Instead, he should have God's Word proclaimed to him as an unquestionable authority."

"But how can we fit these two ideas together?" Denny asked.

"The Bible gives us the answer! In Proverbs 26:5-6 it says, 'Answer not a fool according to his folly, lest you be like him. Answer a fool according to his folly lest he be wise in his own eyes.'"

"I see," shouted Denny, "on the one hand we present the truth of the Bible as unquestionable and thereby keep from becoming like the unbeliever. On the other hand, we argue and seek to convince the unbeliever on his own ground. Right?"

"Almost," Chris replied. "We use reason and arguments in both cases but we argue by truth first and then we argue by folly. We present the biblical answer and evidence for the Christian view, and we seek to destroy the unbeliever's self-confidence by using his own ideas against him."

"Let's go see Cindy and David."

As Denny and Chris arrived at the Nogod home, Certain Cindy and David Doubter agreed that they would talk one more time with Denny's friends.

"Denny tells me that you both have trouble believing that Christianity is true," Chris began. "Is there some particular reason why you will not trust Christ as your Lord and Savior?"

"There sure is!" Cindy exclaimed. "I don't even believe that God exists, much less all that stuff about Jesus and the cross. Why should I believe in God?"

"Let me begin by telling you that my reasons for belief in God stem from my commitment to Christ. When I became a Christian I became aware of God's existence in a way I had never been before."

"Yes, but that doesn't answer my question."

"Wait a minute! Give me a chance! I believe that God exists because the Bible says so again and again. In fact, I cannot conceive of the world being as it is apart from God's creative activity. Everywhere I look I see God's handiwork and His power."

"If that's the best you can do, then you're no better off than Benny Bible Banger. You're asking me to believe something that is not reasonable."

"I understand what you're saying. But from my point of view as a Christian, believing in God is very reasonable. Still, I'm not surprised you do not believe; you have committed yourself to thinking independently."

"I don't understand what you mean," Cindy objected. "I just look at the facts and tell what I see."

"Cindy, I am committed to trusting God's Word and depending on God for the answers to my questions, but you are committed to examining and looking at things independently of God's Word. Why don't you believe in God?"

"Because it is unscientific."

"Why do you think being scientific is the way to truth?"

"It's the only way of thinking that makes sense," Cindy replied.

"The way that makes sense to whom?"

"To me!"

"You see, you have set yourself up as the ultimate judge of what is true and false and that's why you will not accept the Christian view of things."

"So what? I may have decided independently to reject Christianity, but you have done the same thing when you decided to believe it. It was your choice and your decision."

"No, it wasn't," insisted Denny. "After I became a Christian I learned that God was the one who chose me first and enabled me to believe Him. I did not choose independently."

"That's what you say because of the Bible. It's not really true."

"You see, once again you object to the Christian view because you seek to reason independently. Let me ask you a question. Why do you think you are independent and able to know truth without submitting to God and the Bible?"

"Because I think all this talk about depending on God is ridiculous," Cindy said.

"Yes, but you believe it is ridiculous because of your commitment to being independent. You arrived at that conclusion on your own."

"So?"

"So you haven't justified your commitment to independence. You have reasoned in a circle saying that you believe you are independent because you believe something you decided independently. No matter what you answer you cannot justify the commitment that undergirds everything you believe."

"The same is true of you," Cindy urged.

"No! I do not claim that I am the ultimate authority. God is the ultimate authority. God is the one who supports my life-commitment. I know that is foolish from your view, but my point is that your view is foolish and inconsistent not just to my view but to your own view as well."

"How is that true?"

"Your commitment to independence is groundless and yet you want to be so scientific and logical. You are unable to escape that dilemma."

"I guess I see your point. Nevertheless, it is still true that belief in God is unscientific. There is no evidence for God."

"Have you been everywhere in the universe at every moment and then outside the universe looking for God?"

"No."

"Then you can't say for sure that science is against Christianity. You cannot know all the evidence and so you can't be sure there is no God."

"I know that science has shown evolution to be true and God cannot exist if evolution is true."

"Evolution is just a theory, and until scientists know all there is to know about everything, we cannot be sure they are understanding correctly what they claim to know. You can't be certain, Cindy. In fact, since you're limited as you are and refuse to depend on God, it is evident you can't be sure of anything. If you want to be sure about something you have to ignore this problem and have blind faith in yourself. You will never truly arrive at certainty."

David Doubter could not remain quiet any longer. "That's what I've been trying to tell you all along, Certain Cindy," he said. "But the thing you don't see, Chris, is that you can't be any more certain than Cindy. We are all unable to get enough evidence to know anything for sure, much less debatable things like God's existence. I guess that's why I'm an agnostic."

"That's not true, David. I know God exists because God has spoken in His Word. He knows everything, and if I depend on Him I can know truly without knowing everything," Chris responded.

"Yes, but we can't be sure that God has really revealed Himself or that He exists. We have to leave that question alone."

"David, your problem is that you want to be a doubter and stay safe from committing yourself one way or another. Yet, you are fully convinced and sure that we must be uncertain. You are just as dogmatic as Certain Cindy."

"I don't see exactly what you mean."

"You do not know enough to know for sure that we must be uncertain about everything. You can't be sure that we cannot know God until you have searched everywhere and know that such knowledge is not possible."

Chris continued saying, "You both are doing the same thing and making the same mistake. Cindy is sure she is right but to be sure she must not deal with the reality of her limited and uncertain knowledge. David is sure that he is right but he has no way of knowing this for sure. You both ignore the plain facts in order to hold your views."

"But you have to admit this is the best we can do," Cindy replied.

"No, I don't," Chris said. "You have the choice of ignoring the problem, going insane, committing suicide, or becoming a Christian. Christ can save you from this futility. He can give you hope and meaning in life, if you will but trust His death and resurrection as sufficient for your salvation. Commit yourself to dependence on Him."

"You've defended your position well," David admitted. "But we have no desire to become Christians."

"Well, the gospel is offered to you. I hope that you will consider the claims of Christ seriously. In John 3:36 Jesus said,'He who believes in the Son has eternal life; but he who does not obey the Son shall not see life, but the wrath of God abides on him.'"

Chris and Denny left the Nogods' home and went to Chris' home where they prayed for the Nogods. Denny was encouraged; he was no longer defenseless. Both he and Chris gained hope that God would move in the Nogods' hearts and turn them to Christ. Until that time, however, Denny and Chris would continue faithful to their Lord and to the defense of the Christian faith.

Richard L. Pratt, Jr., is professor of Old Testament at Reformed Theological Seminary, Orlando campus. He studied at Westminster Theological Seminary, received his M.Div. from Union Theological Seminary, and earned his Th.D. in Old Testament studies from Harvard University. He is the author of numerous books, including *Pray with Your Eyes Open, He Gave Us Stories,* and *Designed for Dignity.*